MARCO

Tips

HONG KONG

MACAU

SOUTH
KOREA

CHINA Shanghai JAPAN

TAIWAN

Guangzhou Tropic of Cancer

MYANMAR Hong Kong *PACIFIC*

LAOS *OCEAN*

THAILAND VIETNAM

CAMBODIA PHILIPPINES

MALAYSIA BRUNEI

SYMBOLS

INSIDER TIP   Insider Tip

★   Highlight

●●●●   Best of ...

☼   Scenic view

⏱ Responsible travel: fair trade principles and the environment respected

PRICE CATEGORIES HOTELS

Expensive   over 1700 HK$

Moderate   850–1700 HK$

Budget   under 850 HK$

The prices are for a double room per night without breakfast

PRICE CATEGORIES RESTAURANTS

Expensive   over 300 HK$

Moderate   150–300 HK$

Budget   under 150 HK$

The prices are for a meal without drinks and expensive specialities

On the cover: Stunning panoramic views and shady paths p. 34 | Typically Cantonese: dim sum p. 59

CONTENTS

Shopping → p. 64

Entertainment → p. 74

Where to stay → p. 80

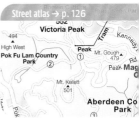

Street atlas → p. 126

DID YOU KNOW?

A 'fragrant harbour' → p. 20
The avoidable cold → p. 22
Relax & Enjoy → p. 33
Keep fit! → p. 39
Books & Films → p. 47
Gambling fever & Rugby
→ p. 52
Gourmet restaurants → p. 58
Local specialities → p. 60
Luxury hotels → p. 84
Fish massage → p. 97
Currency converter → p. 117

MAPS IN THE GUIDEBOOK

(128 A1) Page numbers
and coordinates refer to
the Street atlas
(O) Site/address located off
the map. Coordinates are also
given for places that are not
marked on the Street atlas
Map of surrounding area on
p. 138/139, maps of Macau,
Taipa/Coloane on p. 145–147,
and a public transportation
map inside the back cover

INSIDE BACK COVER:
PULL-OUT MAP →

PULL-OUT MAP

(*A–B 2–3*) Refers to the
removable pull-out map
(*a–b 2–3*) Refers to the
additional inset maps on the
pull-out map

The best MARCO POLO Insider Tips

Our top 15 Insider Tips

INSIDER TIP Full, loud, tasty, fun – yam cha!

Hong Kong's joie-de-vivre is best felt over a dim sum lunch in a teahouse on Sunday – the epitome of the Hong Kong experience → p. 56

INSIDER TIP Enter the fray!

Shopping, dining, watching a film: the Causeway Bay district with its megastores, restaurants and cinemas draws in the crowds after work (photo above) → p. 76

INSIDER TIP Entertaining the gods

The whole island of Cheung Chau celebrates the Bun Festival over three days in honour of its patron saint, the Emperor of the North. Visitors will find all sorts of things to marvel at → p. 108

INSIDER TIP A day at the beach

For example on one of the beaches supervised by lifeguards on car-free Lamma Island. And why not stay overnight at Concerto Inn right on the seafront? → p. 87

INSIDER TIP City lights

The highlight of any stay in Hong Kong: the panorama of the city and harbour from Peak Path is breathtaking at any time but it becomes absolutely overwhelming in the twilight hours → p. 35

INSIDER TIP Trial membership in the Jockey Club

This is possible with the Tourist Badge, and everybody is captivated by the atmosphere of Hong Kong's leading gambling institution – experience it at Happy Valley, Hong Kong's oldest racetrack or at the second track in Sha Tin → p. 38

INSIDER TIP Mountain paths and the roar of the surf

No skyscraper in sight, no car and not even an electricity cable: a day spent hiking to secluded Tai Long Wan Bay – with two wonderful beaches – shows a completely unexpected side of Hong Kong (photo right) → p. 53

INSIDER TIP Marvels of everyday life

That is what visitors discover wandering through the Yau Ma Tei district where they will discover an exotic world far removed from international consumerism → **p. 100**

INSIDER TIP Treasures from the sea and buildings on stilts

You will find both in the fishing village of Lei Yue Mun that can only be explored on foot but is easy to reach by underground → **p. 51**

INSIDER TIP Pilgrimage to the ship shrine

Hong Kong's boatmen receive their blessing for the coming year on the birthday of the 'Empress of Heaven' Tin Hau → **p. 108**

INSIDER TIP Bio-dynamic view of the harbour

Vegetarian food with a panoramic view of the city: the only place to find both is in the chic, but inexpensive, Chinese restaurant Kung Tak Lam in a Kowloon skyscraper → **p. 59**

INSIDER TIP Feel like a colonial gent

You can do that at the afternoon high tea in the magnificient foyer in the famous Peninsula Hotel → **p. 43**

INSIDER TIP Are there really dragons?

Of course there are! And flame-spewing dragons can even be seen dancing in the evening under the full moon during the mid-autumn festival → **p. 109**

INSIDER TIP Sea food, wine and fresh air

... and don't forget a sampan cruise through the labyrinth of islands in Rocky Harbour: an excursion to Sai Kung will show you how relaxing Hong Kong can be → **p. 53**

INSIDER TIP Junk shipyard and Tam Kung Temple

A little church, fine cooking, a small temple and an impressive complex of old shipyards: take a stroll through Colane village on Macau's southernmost island → **p. 90**

BEST OF ...

FOR FREE

● *In the sculpture garden*
You have to pay to see artworks in other places but the modern sculptures in *Kowloon Park* are there for everyone to admire. There is no admission fee here, nor in any of the other parks in Hong Kong → p. 42

● *Dip into history*
Admission to the state museums is free on Wednesdays and none is more fascinating than the *Museum of History*. Whole scenes and buildings have been built on a scale of 1:1 and the sounds and smells will transport visitors back to past times → p. 42

● *A different view of the harbour*
Although the panorama from The Peak is incomparable, the view from the rooftop of the *IFC Mall* is easier to reach and free of charge. Here, you are much closer to the harbour with the excitement of all the shipping taking place and surrounded by the glittering atmosphere of the skyscrapers in the metropolis (photo) → p. 31

● *Zoological and Botanical Gardens*
You can experience all that Hong Kong's *Zoological and Botanical Gardens* have to offer free of charge. The main attractions in the well cared for, shady complex with occasional views of the city's maze of skyscrapers are the elegant ibises and the orangutans → p. 36

● *Discover classical China in a convent*
There is no charge for the Buddhist *Chi Lin Nunnery*, built in a style that dates back more than 1100 years ago, with golden effigies and the wonderful Nan Lian Garden that is part of the complex → p. 47

● *Experience the Grand Prix*
If you missed out on seeing the Macau Grand Prix race 'live', you can learn all about its history and even have a thrilling driving experience in the *Grand Prix Museum* – and it won't cost a penny → p. 92

○○○○ Dots in guidebook refer to 'Best of ...' tips

● *Cruise the harbour*

Take the *Star Ferry* – Hong Kong's number one traditional means of transport! It lost its importance
after the construction of the underground, but
there is no nicer way to get from Tsim Sha Tsui
to Wan Chai or Central than with the chubby
boats that can travel both forwards and
backwards (photo) → p. 27

● *City tour for next to nothing*

With the *tram* – the number two traditional means of transport! No other way
of getting an idea of life in Hong Kong is
more comfortable, less expensive and more
characteristic than from the top deck as the
tram makes its way through canyons of the high
buildings on Hong Kong Island → p. 26

● *Get to the top*

With the help of the *Peak Tram* – transport institution number three!
At the very latest, you will realise that it was a good idea to come to
Hong Kong when you see the spectacular panorama opening up before
your eyes as the tram climbs higher and higher → p. 35

● *Buy t-shirts, consult a fortune teller …*

… or listen to operatic arias. The evening market on *Temple Street* offers
this and much, much more every night. And, of course, it is also another Hong Kong institution! → p. 79

● *Try dim sums*

One of the best places to try these typical Cantonese delicacies accompanied by tea is *Maxim's Palace* in City Hall where foreigners are especially welcome. The most typical day is Sunday when it is especially
loud and tumultuous → p. 59

● *Sacrifice to the gods*

In the *Wong Tai Sin Temple,* the most popular in Hong Kong, you will
discover just how very alive religion has remained for those living in
this apparently westernised, materialistic city → p. 49

● *One-armed bandits and baroque paintings*

Macau, the Las Vegas of the East, offers this strange combination in its
craziest casino-hotel-theatre-shopping mall: *The Venetian* on Cotai → p. 91

ONLY IN

BEST OF ...

● **Stay dry in Central**
How can you get around in the *Central District* without getting wet even though it's raining and you don't have an umbrella? Covered pedestrian bridges make it possible for you to walk for miles and you are even under cover on the Central Escalator → **p. 28**

● **Experience art**
The *Museum of Art* is probably the best place to admire beautiful things when it's wet outside. The collection of exquisite ancient and modern art more than makes up for the moods of the weather → **p. 42**

● **Eleven floors of window shopping**
Or could there be twelve? In any case, the shopping delights under a roof in *Times Square* stretch from several floors below ground level to the 9th floor above. And, if you feel hungry, you won't have to go outside to have a bite to eat either (photo) → **p. 67**

● **Pretend to be a millionaire**
Do it in the lobby of the *Mandarin Oriental*. Relaxing over a cup of English tea is the perfect way to while away your time. You can people watch, read a bit and enjoy the luxurious surroundings without it costing the earth → **p. 84**

● **Stroll through Macau's history**
Macau is proud of its history and you will be able to experience its essence at *Macau Museum* – much of it on a 1:1 scale! There is more than enough to keep you busy for at least two rainy hours → **p. 94**

● **Dreaming**
At least that's what the name of the *City of Dreams* in Macau promises. The Dragon's Treasure Show in the *Bubble Cinema* will certainly make that happen and you can also dream about winning in the casino – and why not finish off by visiting 'The House of Dancing Water' Show? → **p. 91**

RAIN

RELAX AND CHILL OUT
Take it easy and spoil yourself

● *Be kneaded*
There are many places offering foot massages in Hong Kong but *Iyara* has much more to make you feel good – going as far as treatments lasting for hours – and that in an amazingly central location near the Central Escalator → **p. 33**

● *Time for tea*
The Cantonese tea culture in Hong Kong can be best experienced at a tasting session in the *Lok Cha Tea Shop*. The friendly atmosphere and tranquillity will help you enjoy your rest → **p. 73**

● *Lie on the deck of a junk*
Prop your head up and, gently swaying, let the panorama of Hong Kong's skyscrapers drift past you. You will find a tour on the renovated junk *Duk Ling* one of the most peaceful ways to see the city and the harbour → **p. 119**

● *Dim sum nostalgia*
The typical teahouse in Hong Kong is large and noisy; *Dim Sum* on the other hand is small, refined and nostalgic – a place to enjoy a quiet life even though it can be crowded and a bit louder at lunchtime → **p. 58**

● *Laze on the beach*
There are many possibilities to do this in Hong Kong. *Repulse Bay* is the easiest beach to reach. There is nothing lovelier than lying on one of the pontoons being gently rocked by the waves. And then: just close your eyes, feel the water and sun caressing your skin and imagine you are in the South Seas → **p. 48**

● *Feed the cleaner fish*
At the *Fish Spa* in Macau, you put your arms in warm water and leave the peeling up to the fish – a very special feel-good experience → **p. 97**

INTRODUCTION

DISCOVER HONG KONG!

There is no doubt about it. Hong Kong is a synonym for the fascination of the Far East. Everybody has a certain picture in their mind. On the one hand, one expects an extremely modern, international metropolis whose economic dynamism manifests itself in a forest of skyscrapers and where the wealthy are chauffeured around in Rolls Royces. On the other hand, visitors hope to experience the exotic atmosphere of China, the enigmatic, the unfamiliar. And, you would not be really far off there either. This Chinese metropolis with 155 years of British tradition is both cosmopolitan and fascinatingly different. Here, the Chinese has been moulded by the British, striving for profit has been amalgamated with traditional Chinese values and the liberal economic atmosphere and work discipline go hand in hand with culture and pleasure. The only thing you should forget is the cliché about the city being a stronghold of criminality and secret societies. Things in Hong Kong are much more orderly than in many large European cities.

The first time you visit Hong Kong, you will find coming to grips with the city somewhat challenging. The pushing and shoving on the streets, the smell of exhaust fumes from

Photo: View from The Peak

cars in the canyons between high buildings, the noise of the swarms of buses, cement mixers and pneumatic drills reverberating off the façades of the high-rises in this incessantly hectic city. Some visitors are even happy to leave after only two days of shopping and a single city tour.

A Chinese metropolis, cosmopolitan and fascinatingly different

Of course, they won't have missed out on palaces or romantic ruins, famous museums or charming squares. Hong Kong's records are much more sober: Asia's second-largest financial metropolis (after Tokyo), the highest shop rentals in the world, the underground with the world's largest transport volume per kilometre, the globe's third-largest container port and some of the highest skyscrapers on earth. But the truth is: Hong Kong itself is a unique attraction with its contrasting mountains and water, its skyscrapers and its culinary delights. It almost seems to be a miracle that this capitalist eldorado on the doorstep of the Chinese giant can function at all – on a problematic piece of land suitable for just about anything but being the site of a metropolis with a population of around seven million.

At the beginning, this location south of the Tropic of Cancer was missing all the prerequisites for such a success story. When the British occupied the island as one of the spoils of war in 1841, they planned to establish a military base and not a large city. It

Trade and change in Hong Kong: Times Square Shopping centre in the Causeway Bay district

soon became clear that there was a serious lack of building space and land in the surrounding area that could sustain a rapidly growing town. At the time, Viscount Palmerstone – speaking at Westminster – said that Hong Kong was just 'a barren island with hardly a house upon it'. And that is why the British expanded their booty twice: in 1860 to include the Kowloon Peninsula – ceded 'for eternity', just like

> **'A barren island with hardly a house upon it'**

the island – and, in 1898, the neighbouring section of the mainland and additional islands that were then leased for 99 years and today make up around 90 percent of the total surface area of 425 square miles. Hong Kong's connection to the hinterland remained poor until about 1980 – and that not only because of the border.

From the outset, Hong Kong's main *raison d'être* was as a place to do business, and many Chinese knew how to profit from that; they left their homeland that was reeling from one crisis to the next and started to settle in Hong Kong soon after its foundation. The greatest flood of migrants took place during the Civil War and the emergence of the Communists (1945–49). Soon, the slopes of the hills were covered with gigantic settlements for poor people. The most pressing task was to create social housing in order to prevent the colony from falling into chaos – but where could space be found for that? Efforts to create new land on embankments had already begun in the 19th century; Queen's Road, the first to be built along the shore, is now up to

650m (2000ft) from the water. In the meantime, entire bays have disappeared and mountains moved, and Hong Kong is still expanding several square miles every year. Above all, new towns had to be built in the rural New Territories where almost half of Hong Kong's 7.1 million inhabitants live today.

Outsiders might not find these skyscraper settlements particularly attractive but there is no alternative, especially not for those living there, many of whom experienced – at first hand – life in the slums that have now disappeared. The European luxury cars you will see on the parking levels in many of these skyscraper complexes is proof that the people living there are often amazingly wealthy. On the other hand, the 'housing cages' frequently talked about in Europe, that elderly unemployed people are sqeezed into, are only a peripheral phenomenon. The art of coping with a lack of space is, however, something that

One of Hong Kong's 263 islands, perfect for a day's outing: Cheung Chau

almost everybody in everybody in Hong Kong has to come to terms, with the exception of the extremely wealthy who live in villas.

The second major challenge facing Hong Kong was its traffic problem. The Territory consists of 263 islands and even the large section on the mainland is broken up by peninsulas, mountains and deep bays. Things improved considerably after 1980 with the introduction of the underground and its many tunnels. Today, there are more than 20 miles of road tunnels in addition to elevated bridges with a total length of over 12km (7½mi).

> **The Territory is a place of unbelievable contrasts**

The third problem was the lack of drinking water; it even had to be rationed in years when the rainfall was poor. Today, the supply is guaranteed by two gigantic reservoirs that have been wrested from the sea, as well as water pipes from China. The fourth problem was the easiest on to solve: unemployment. There was plenty of experience in making money. In addition, Hong Kong had taken over Shanghai's function as the Chinese trade, production and finance centre in 1949 and developed into China's almost sole door to the outside world – a lucrative source of revenue for the capitalistic enclave. However, in the 1990s, almost all of the industry moved back across the border into China and now many of the people of Hong Kong commute to work in Shenzhen.

Today, the territory is a place of incredible contrasts. Cutting-edge technology and Chinese traditions, metropolis and secluded mountains, noise and tranquillity – all of this tightly packed together. Offerings of oranges and incense are made to the God of Doors, the Earth and Prosperity in a small metal shrine next to the entrance of a sophisticated nightclub with hi-tech equipment. Fashionably dressed office workers with their mobile phones go to the cemetery to tend to the graves of their ancestors and a subtropical jungle, where colourful butterflies flutter around during the day and crickets chirp at night, starts immediately behind the last 25-storey skyscraper.

The most dominant feeling however is one of the city's dynamism and its talent for being able to realise ideas and plans in no time. The latest fashions can be found on the shelves here long before they have even been unpacked in Europe. But the times when Hong Kongers worked from the early hours of the morning until late at night and their only pleasure was an occasional evening playing mahjong have now gone. The city has developed into a pleasure metropolis – especially for gourmets. It is absolutely normal to go out to eat and consumers indulge themselves in the gigantic shopping malls. But the passion with which two traditional vices are cultivated has remained unbroken: horse racing and gambling in neighbouring Macau.

View from The Peak: the panorama is Hong Kong's greatest marvel

Macau! A visit to the oldest European outpost in the Far East is normally a part of any trip to Hong Kong. The small territory, which was returned to China in 1999 – a good two years after Hong Kong – is in no way just a miniature version of its formerly British counterpart at the mouth of the Pearl River. Even though today the gigantic gambling casinos attract most tourists to Macau and have made it famous as Asia's Las Vegas, there are many more testimonies to its centuries-long past as a Portuguese colony here than through the much shorter British presence in Hong Kong.

Many visitors feel that both cities have become completely westernised; but this impression fades away if you look closer. Of course, many British elements have been preserved since Hong Kong's 'return': the currency, bilingualism, the judicial system, visa-free entry and the border to the new mother, and old father, country. Thoroughfares such as Queen's Road and Prince Edward Road have also kept their old names. But only a minority speaks more-or-less good English. The skyscrapers are 'homemade' and constructed with the help of traditional bamboo scaffolding. And family solidarity is still of the utmost importance. The city and people living in it are modern and enthusiastic about the latest technology but it would be a mistake to think that everything that is not old-Chinese is western.

As you wander through the labyrinth of skyscrapers, you will be amazed at the high level of social order. The spotless underground is absolutely safe and there are no signs of graffiti. Travel out to the islands, hike over the hills, explore the beaches. Relish the seafood and all of the other delicacies the local restaurants have to offer. The first two days in Hong Kong are always terrible. Stay for seven days and you will want to extend for another week. If you really only have half a day, travel to The Peak. The magnificent panorama will show you what the city and people living there have to – and have – overcome. That is the real Hong Kong miracle. You can buy silk blouses when you get home.

WHAT'S HOT

1 Tea Time

Where old meets new In Hong Kong, tea joins forces with modern ingredients. Mixed with fruit milk, juice or jelly balls, the aromatic brew makes itself fit for the future. So-called Bubble or Pearl Tea is served in the cool environment of the *Xiang Zong Lin Teahouses (e.g. Pioneer Centre, 270 Nathan Rd.).* You will also be able to try the unusually beverage, which originated in Taiwan, in the *Saint's Alp Teahouse (in The Westwood, Belcher's Street).*

Young and wild

Fashion Hong Kong is crazy about the latest fashion trends. That makes competitions for up-and-coming designers, such as the *Hong Kong Fashion Week (www.hktdc.com),* so important. Talents including *Mountain Yam (mountainyam.com, photo)* and Eva Cheng Yee Wah *(aevacheng.blogspot.com),* who is so admired for her use of the traditional Chinese silhouette technique, were discovered and promoted here. Cony Ko makes appropriate accessories – using natural materials *(Taka, 16A Aberdeen St.).*

3 Skyline surfing

Action Similar to wakeboarding, wakeskating takes place on a board on the water. The view of the megacity from the sea makes it even more exciting. Beginners start in Tai Tam Bay *(www.wakeboard.com.hk)* or take a few lessons form Dewey, the wake teacher who also owns a shop *(17 Po Chong Wan, Shum Wan Rd., www.wakeboarding.com.hk, photo).* You can buy wakeskate equipment and the suitable outfits from *Island Wake (3 Cannon St., www.islandwake.com).*

There are a lot of things to discover in Hong Kong. A few of the most interesting are listed below

Artistic city

Great and small Young creative artists no longer just want to show their works in established museums but in the hip lounges and mini-galleries that are so popular in the art world – one is *Para/Site*, the smallest gallery in town. There is very little space and this makes it even more sought after. Even Joo Choon-Lin showed her chocolate bears here *(4 Po Yan St., www. para-site.org.hk, photo)*. *1a space*, on the other hand, is much roomier. The artists' collective has taken over an old industrial area where it organises artistic happenings, performances and exhibitions *(Unit 4, Cattle Depot Artist Village, 63 Ma Tau Kok Rd., www. oneaspace.org.hk)*. The *Living Room Craft Fair* does not even have a fixed location. This art market wanders from one place to the next *(dates under www.facebook.com/group. php?gid=67867131022)*.

Garden city

Greenery It is also green in the megacity. The people of Hong Kong have discovered the joys of nature and even grow their own fruit and vegetables. You can rent a patch from the *Hong Kong Flower World* for this purpose and can also improve your gardening skills at special workshops on proper pruning and fertilising *(232 Tai Kong Po, Kam Tin, www.flowerworldhk. com)*. A visit to the *Simply Organic Farm (113 Ho Pui, Pat Heung)* will help budding gardeners; they can also buy fresh, crisp organic products in the farm shop in the city *(21 Canal Rd. West, www.organic-farm.com)*.

IN A NUTSHELL

BAUHINIA

The purplish-red blossom of the bauhinia tree is Hong Kong's flower and – in white – adorns the city's flag. This is the specially cultivated variety 'blakeana' named after a former governor. It flowers from November to March and can be admired on many of the city's promenades and squares.

China presented Hong Kong with a golden bauhinia flower upon its 'return' in 1997; together with its base, the bronze statue is 6m (18ft) high and has been placed on the harbour side of the Convention and Exhibition Centre in Wan Chai.

CANTONESE

Nowhere else is this South Chinese dialect spoken as widely as it is in Hong Kong. It is not only the main language of communication but also the second official language after English. The difference between Cantonese and standard Chinese is at least as great as between Spanish and Portuguese or Dutch and German. Standard Chinese is the norm in the written language but many popular newspapers use special Cantonese slang characters that other Chinese do not understand. Standard Chinese was not even taught in schools until the 1990s. However, it has now become impossible for a Hong

Photo: Hiking trail on Hong Kong Island

Patron Saint and opium: Some background information on what to expect in the Special Administrative Area of Hong Kong

Konger to have contacts with his clients – in the retail trade or gastronomy – without knowledge of Standard Chinese. Announcements on the underground are made in three languages: first in Cantonese, then Standard Chinese and finally in English.

COUNTRY PARKS

It is hard to believe if you do not know Hong Kong well: there is so much green

land that it is possible to go on mountain hikes lasting for days. This is the due to the *24 Country Parks*, landscape conservation areas that were established after 1976 to protect the city's water reserves. They are spread over Hong Kong Island, Lantau and the mainland and consist of partly wooded, partly grassy, hilly terrain. Hikers will be pleased to find well-marked paths, camping sites, shelters, barbecue areas, information boards and visitors' centres that provide details on the flora and fauna. Four main trails lead to the most beautiful places; some sections can be reached by bus. You might come across snakes so make sure you wear sturdy shoes!

Further information is available under *www.gov.hk/en/residents/culture/trail* as well as *www.afcd.gov.hk/eindex.html*; the best maps can be obtained from the *Publications Sales Unit, 4/F, Murray Building, Garden Rd., Central, tel. 25 37 19 10* (133 E3) *(🗺 C12)*.

FENG SHUI

This Chinese term means 'wind and water' and stands for unseen influences in the vicinity that can have an effect on buildings or a grave and, if they are adverse, can lead to poverty, illness and infertility. To make sure this does not occur, a feng shui master is consulted before building begins and he gets down to work with a special compass. However, no feng shui master has ever prevented a building being constructed. Profits always take first place! Small details are corrected: the entrance moved a little, the decoration of the façade changed or a mirror attached to the outside to ward off evil.

A block of flats on Repulse Bay in particular is often referred to when illustrating the significance of feng shui. The number of privately-owned flats was reduced to be able to incorporate a large hole in a building to make sure that the dragon living on the mountain could still see the sea. However, it is difficult not to suspect that this was actually a marketing gag.

GAMBLING AND HORSE RACING

Every lotto player knows the thrill of challenging Fortuna, the goddess of luck. She is unknown in Hong Kong but this has no effect on the passion people feel about the possibility of making loads of money with just a small wager. There are two legal ways to do this in Hong Kong: to bet at the racetrack or play mahjong. The popularity of horse racing can only really be explained by the fact that you can bet. The never-ending flow of income has made the Hong Kong Jockey Club the Area's most financially potent charitable institution. But, Macau is the place to go if you want to really live your passion for gambling to the utmost. This former Portuguese overseas province has developed into the world's largest heaven on earth for gamblers – mainly due to the nouveau riche from the mainland, many of them government officials made wealthy through corruption. Mahjong, on the other hand,

A 'FRAGRANT HARBOUR'

When the British first came to Hong Kong, they bunkered fresh water at a dock near Aberdeen where agar-wood, one of the raw materials used for making incense, was traded. When asked the name of the place, the local sailors answered in their dialect: 'Hong Kong', incense harbour. However, the British thought that this was the name of the entire island and wrongly translated the *hong* (Cantonese *höng*, Standard Chinese *xiang*) which can mean both 'fragrance' and 'incense' with *fragrant*. This misunderstanding was only cleared up a good 140 years later but still stubbornly persists.

is usually played at home with four people taking part. There are special mahjong tables of just the right size with a drawer for each player to keep his winnings and bets; mahjong without the added attraction of winning would be 'kids' stuff'. Things are a bit more serious in the mahjong salons. But even there, the bets are not very high; if they were, winnings would be taxed.

solar year. The Chinese lunar year always begins with the first full moon after 21 January. As a rule, there is more activity in the temples at new moon and full moon than at other times. That is when offerings of money are also burned in red metal buckets on the roadside.

Win or place? Suspense at the Happy Valley Racetrack

LUNAR CALENDAR

Most of China's traditional festivities are based on the moon calendar with a 354 or 355-day year. It is actually a moon-and-sun calendar because every 33 to 35 months an intercalary month is added at the beginning of the year to adapt it to the

OPIUM WAR

If the British had not been so fond of tea 200 years ago, Hong Kong would probably not exist today. Tea came from China but trade was a one-way street: the Middle Kingdom did not buy anything from the British until they came up with the idea of drug smuggling. The business of trafficking with Indian opium flourished. More and more Chinese became addicted and more silver left China than came in through exporting tea. The Emperor sent an incorruptible official to Canton: Lin Zexu. In 1839, he had all of the opium stored in Canton destroyed. Great Britain considered this a declaration of war and the first Opium War began. With the Nanking Peace treaty in 1842, China was forced to open four additional ports to overseas trade and cede the island of Hong Kong to the British Crown 'in perpetuity'. 18 years later, in the second Opium War, Kowloon (as far as Boundary Street) was added, followed in 1898 by the lease of the New Territories.

ORACLES AND FORTUNE TELLING

The simplest and cheapest form of an oracle can often be seen in temples: the person seeking advice holds two kidney-shaped pieces of wood in his or her hand, moves them up and down in front of the altar and silently implores the appropriate god before throwing them onto the ground. Depending on whether their round or flat side lies on the bottom, this can mean 'yes', 'no' or 'maybe'. The stick oracle is the appropriate form for more complicated matters. A box with numbered sticks is shaken until one falls out; the temple's fortune teller then looks up the number in a book and interprets the saying in keeping with the concern the believer has. Physiognomers, who tell the future from a person's face and chiromancers who do the same by looking at the lines on your palms often work together with a temple. Trained birds are also used as oracles; they pull a saying out of a heap of papers.

POPULATION

Only 5% of the population is made up of foreigners and this makes Hong Kong less international than many cities in Europe. The largest minority group comes from the Philippines (2.1%) – mainly women who work as domestic helps – followed by Indonesians (0.8%) and around 19,000 British (0.3%). Cantonese is the mother tongue of 85% of the 7.1 million people living in Hong Kong.

After the Japanese, the Hong Kongers have the longest life expectancy in the world: close to 80 years for newly-born males and 86 for females. Almost half of the population lives in houses provided by the government housing authority. About 40% of those employed work in trade, including gastronomy; the second largest professional group works in the banking and insurance sectors (20%).

RELIGION

Christians of various confessions make up around 8% of the population. Moslems (Chinese, Indonesians and Pakistanis) account for a little more than 1%. The majority still adhere to the extremely lively, popular Chinese religion. The faithful worship Buddhist and Taoist deities alongside each other; the most important

THE AVOIDABLE COLD

There is no restaurant owner who wants to have a reputation for skimping on air-conditioning of all things. You'll always arrive dripping in sweat which will feel like an icy shower down your back after 15 mins. By the third day at the latest you'll have a streaming cold. So always take a cardigan or pullover with you!

thing is to choose the god who will listen to your prayers and then give you the help you need.

Most of the around 200 temples in Hong Kong were built in the 19th century. They are often small buildings with a single room. Larger temple complexes were not erected until after 1950. The faithful come to pray or question the oracle. They give added weight to the wishes they make to the gods and thank them with offerings of incense, fruit and money. Each temple has at least one main deity: it is usually placed in a gilded shrine behind the altar with incense burners, vases, lamps and offerings. Some temples have litters that were used to carry the effigy during processions. Coils of incense hang from the roof; a piece of paper in the middle lists the donor's wishes. Furnished houses, litters, cars and servants made of coloured paper are burned and sent to the hereafter as gifts for the dead.

The most popular temple gods are: *Guan Yin* (Cantonese: Kwun Yum), the female Bodhisattva of mercy; *Guan Yu* (Kwun Kung), the god of war and patron saint of many professions – many shops and restaurants have a shrine to him; *Tian Hou* (Tin Hau, 'Empress of Heaven'), the protector of sailors – there are about 25 temples dedicated to this goddess in Hong Kong. But the most esteemed is the god of wealth, doors and the earth; his small shrine is often placed near the ground next to the door.

You will be able to get an idea of ancestral worship at the festivals in honour of the dead, if you visit one of the ancestral temples that still exist in some clan villages or in the memorial halls, such as the one in the Man Mo Temple, where places for ancestral tablets can be purchased. You should walk anticlockwise in a temple and not forget to leave a small donation when you leave.

SAR

With the 'return' of the territory to the People's Republic of China in 1997, the former colony became a Special

Bronze Buddha in the Po Lin Monastery on Lantau Island

Administrative Region. The juridical foundation was the British-Chinese agreement reached in 1984 granting Hong Kong a special status until the year 2047. There is a similar arrangement with the SAR Macau: the former Portuguese colony was handed back to China in December 1999.

THE PERFECT DAY
Hong Kong in 24 hours

07:00am MORNING SPORT AND YAM CHA!

Hong Kong awakens to gymnastics in the morning – a Chinese tradition that you can experience in many places including *Victoria Park* → p. 39. Then it's time for *yam cha* (a cup of tea): Hong Kong breakfast with dim sums in *Crystal Jade* → p. 58 which opens its doors at 7.30am. You have 45 minutes to relax before catching the tram to Statue Square.

09:00am OFF TO THE ISLAND

A walk of a little over half a mile will take you to the ferry at Pier 5. You have to catch the 9 o'clock ferry to *Cheung Chau* → p. 49 (photo, left) (Sat/Sun: 9.30am), travel time one hour, and then tour the island until noon. A good place to have lunch is the *So Bor Kee (Pak She Praya Rd. 11C, Budget)*. The return trip starts at 1.15pm (Sat/Sun 1.30pm).

02:15pm A STROLL IN THE FINANCIAL CENTRE

Back at Pier 5 – and its time to tackle the big city! You will see the skyscrapers of the *International Finance Centre* → p. 30 towering up in front of you with the elegant IFC Mall in between them. Browse the shops for the latest fashions and then go up to the roof. After that, treat youself to a cup of coffee in *Café Costa* (on Lane Crawford). Cross over the pedestrian bridge to the Central Market and continue until you reach the Central Escalator.

04:00pm PUT YOUR LEGS UP

Had enough walking? Take the escalator up one floor and keep your eyes open for *Iyara* → p. 33 on the left. Be sure to book a 30-minute foot massage in advance. Then it's off to the next tram stop (past the Central Market, then to the left). You can take any tram travelling east. Get off at the fifth stop!

05:00pm UP TO THE PEAK

Go into the Pacific Place Shopping Centre (photo, centre) and straight to the escalator up to *Hong Kong Park* → p. 32 (photo, right). Now you should time everything exactly so that you catch the sunset. Go straight to the lower terminal of the *Peak Tram* → p. 35. If you do this at the weekend, you will probably have to wait so shorten the programme by about 30 minutes. And now you float upwards to the highlight of any trip to Hong Kong: the *panorama of the city in twilight* → p. 35. Split your dinner in two: anybody who visits The Peak should not miss out on the *Peak Lookout* → p. 63 (if sunset is late, stop off here first). After a starter and glass of wine, take the Peak Tram down the hill, catch the 15C bus to the Star Ferry and cross over to the other side.

08:00pm LASER SHOW AND HARBOUR LIGHTS

The next highlight: the *Symphony of Lights* → p. 76. The view of the illuminated skyscrapers (some with changing colours) and dazzling billboards even makes the view from the Avenue of Stars worthwhile before or after the laser show.

08:30pm DINNER WITH A VIEW

Dinner, part 2: you can eat a light, healthy, not very expensive vegetarian Chinese meal in *Kung Tak Lam* → p. 59. Important: don't forget to book – preferably one day in advance. Then you will have the chance of getting a table with a view of the harbour!

10:00pm BARGAIN HUNTING AND OPERATIC ARIAS

No visit to Hong Kong would be complete without the *Temple Street night market* → p. 79. This is not only a dream world for bargain hunters. You can also listen to Chinese opera arias and consult a fortune teller near the Tin Hau Temple.

02:45am PANORAMIC DRINK

Now you can fritter away all the money you saved on Temple Street – you will need it to finance a nightcap to end the day in *Aqua Spirit* → p. 76, a bar with stunning panoramic views. After that, everybody will be more than ready for bed.

Train to the starting point: MTR
Stop: Causeway Bay
The Octopus Card with HK$100 credit is very practical (can also be topped up)!

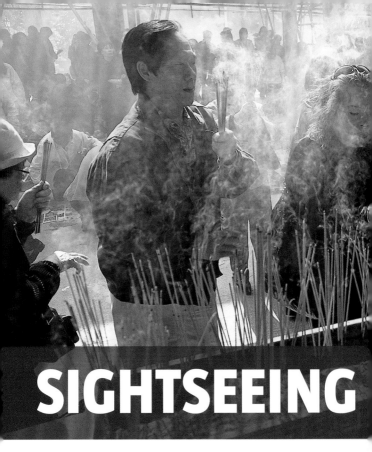

SIGHTSEEING

CITY **WHERE TO START?**
Statue Square **(133 E3)**
(Ø C11): the central point in the Central District with the historical Legco Building and the elegant Mandarin Oriental Hotel. The tram stops at the south end; four underground lines converge here and a network of footbridges provides access to a large part of Central leading northwards to the gigantic tower of the International Finance Centre with its shopping mall and view of the harbour and ferry terminals.

Don't worry about the heat, rain and sultry atmosphere! You will not have to walk very far to discover the real Hong Kong – the modern city as well as the traditional districts such as Yau Ma Tai and Sheung Wan.

The parks provide peaceful areas to catch your breath, the shopping centres cool air and the museums will broaden your horizons – but those who want to experience the city sitting down instead of sweating can take a nostalgic means of transportation: the ● *tram* has connected the districts in the north of the island with each other since 1904 **(133 D2–135 F1)** *(Ø A–H 10–12)*, and the chubby boats of

Between The Peak and the harbour: palatial banks and temples blackened with incense – and much more waiting to be discovered

the ● *Star Ferry Line* have chugged their way between Tsim Sha and Central since 1898 (130 B6, 133 E2) (*m D9, C11*).

A visit to a museum is not merely a good idea when it's raining. Although they are not world-famous, many of them are well worth a visit. Generous benefactors have donated wonderful artistic treasures and the exemplary methods of presentation make a foreign culture accessible to visi-

tors to these government-run institutions. A ticket costing HK$30 and valid for one week provides admission to the Museum of Art, Museum of History, the Science Museum, the Space Museum and several more. Others, including the Medicine, Police, and Railway Museums are described in the brochure 'Hong Kong Cultural Kaleidoscope' available from the Hong Kong Tourism Board (HKTB).

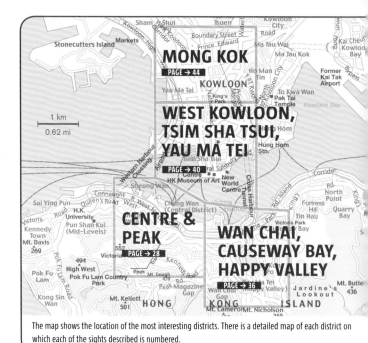

The map shows the location of the most interesting districts. There is a detailed map of each district on which each of the sights described is numbered.

It is easy to reach more distant locations on the speedy, air-conditioned trains operated by the MTR underground as well the Kowloon-Canton railway. However, the crowning highlight is always the cable car trip to The Peak.

CENTRE & PEAK

中環, 山頂

This is the nucleus of the former Crown Colony; this is where the British flag was raised for the first time.

And this is where the city, which was named Victoria at the time, was built along and above Queen's Road (both named after Queen Victoria); it was the forerunner of today's Central District that, together with the neighbouring Admiralty District, forms the heart of Hong Kong's commercial life. Visitors reach some of the oldest, most colourful and most densely populated districts to the west and east; as you proceed upwards, things become greener, more elegant and much more expensive.

● *Central District:* Here, you can walk for miles over bridges and wander through buildings without ever going down to street level. Hong Kong's 'front room', overshadowed by the Hong Kong Bank, is ★ *Statue Square* (133 E3) (*∅ C11*). This is where Filipino maids living in the city organise a gigantic picnic every Sunday. The oldest section of Central with the

Central Market (133 D2) (*㎡ C11*), which is currently being revamped for a different purpose, is on the west side of the square; from here the almost 880m (2890ft)-long *Central Escalator* whisks people up to the Mid-levels residential area. Since the 1970s, earth has been filled into the area north of Connaught Road to create building land. The 420m (1378ft)-high tower of the *International Finance Centre* towers up like an enormous exclamation mark. The *City Hall*, with rooms for all kinds of events, is located on what was once the shoreline on Edinburgh Place to the north-east of the square. The *Admiralty* office district (formerly naval parade grounds) with the Bank of China Tower follows on the eastern side. Central is dominated by The Peak, the villa district with Hong Kong's main attraction: the panoramic view of the harbour and city.

Sheung Wan is to the west of Central (132 C2) (*㎡ B10–11*). In spite of the encroaching office buildings, a feeling for Hong Kong's exotic flair has survived here. The highlights are listed in Walk No. 3.

The most comfortable place to get an impression of life in the north of the island (reaching to the east far beyond Causeway Bay) is from the top of the tram. The double-decker carriages, which also serve as mobile advertisement hoardings, are considered attractions in their own right. You will have no trouble getting one of the best seats at the front of the upper deck if you catch the tram at a terminus such as the one at Western Market. The lines to Shau Kei Wan and Kennedy Town are the longest; the ones to Happy Valley end in a drab branch line.

■1■ BANK OF CHINA TOWER 中銀大廈
(133 E3) (*㎡ D12*)

The new building of the Chinese National Bank is also a political monument. The 368m (1207ft)-high tower was the tallest building on earth when completed in 1990 and was intended to symbolise China's

---

★ **Statue Square**
The square with a view of the bank towers is the heart of Hong Kong
→ p. 28

★ **Hong Kong Park**
An oasis of greenery in the skyscraper jungle
→ p. 32

★ **Peak Trail**
Breathtaking panorama of the city → p. 35

★ **Museum of Art**
Cultural treasures from China and modern art from Hong Kong → p. 42

★ **Museum of History**
A revelation for museum-haters
→ p. 42

★ **Mong Kok**
The city's market place – with pedestrian precincts
→ p. 44

★ **Ocean Park**
A trip in a gondola and dolphin show with a view of the ocean in Hong Kong's best amusement park
→ p. 47

★ **Stanley**
Hong Kong's southernmost district attracts visitors with its clothes market, promenade and Maritime Museum
→ p. 48

★ **Wong Tai Sin Temple**
Offerings and fortune tellers → p. 49

★ **Lantau and Po Lin Monastery**
Long beaches and a giant Buddha on Hong Kong's largest island
→ p. 50

MARCO POLO HIGHLIGHTS

territorial claim to the colony. However, it only held the record for two years. The bank occupies just part of the building designed by the Chinese-American architect Ieoh Ming Pei, which was also intended to be a sign of China's modernisation and opening to the 'West'. However it met with a certain amount of disapproval as it ignored the rules of *feng shui* (geomancy) that the Communists consider a superstition. With its sharp angles, the building does appear to be out of place here. The fortress-like base with its battlements is the complete opposite to the openness demonstrated by the Hong Kong Bank Building. *Corner Queensway 金鐘道/Garden Rd. | MTR Admiralty*

☑ CENTRAL POLICE STATION
前中區警署 (133 D3) *(𝄞 B–C11)*

The former main police station (complete with prison) forms the largest ensemble of colonial-style buildings to have been preserved in Hong Kong. They were built between 1864 and 1925. Currently, discussions are being held on their conversion and there are plans to establish a mixture of restaurants, a museum and art gallery. *Corner Hollywood Rd. 荷李活道/Arbuthnot Rd.*

☑ EXCHANGE SQUARE 交易廣場 AND INTERNATIONAL FINANCE CENTRE 國際金融中心
(133 D–E2) *(𝄞 C11)*

Construction of the two towers of the Stock Exchange (Exchange Square) with their elegant, distinguished-looking façades of mirrored glass and pink-coloured Spanish marble was completed in 1985. The plaza with fountains and sculptures in front of the building is actually on the roof of a bus terminus and leads into the main portal with escalators taking visitors up to the foyer where art exhibitions are also shown. The building was the architectural highlight on the harbour front of Central for 15 years but has now become overshadowed by Tower 2 of the International Finance Centre (IFC). This pleasant-looking building was designed by Cesar Pelli but its height of 420m (1378ft) spoils both the view of The

A reflection of the times: the futuristic glass palaces on Exchange Square

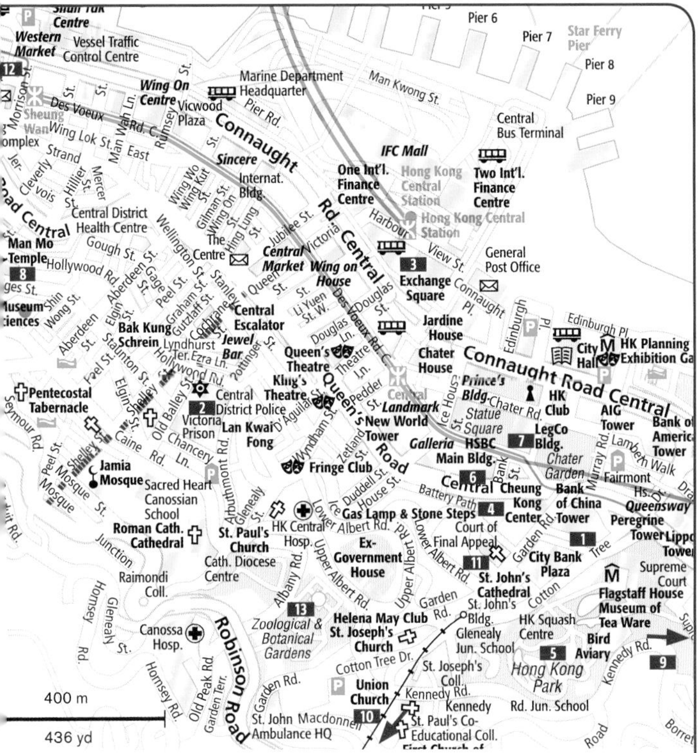

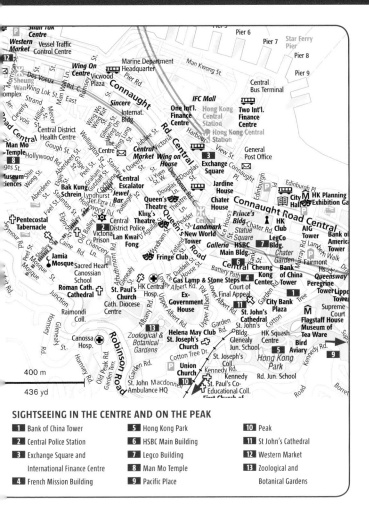

SIGHTSEEING IN THE CENTRE AND ON THE PEAK

1 Bank of China Tower
2 Central Police Station
3 Exchange Square and International Finance Centre
4 French Mission Building
5 Hong Kong Park
6 HSBC Main Building
7 Legco Building
8 Man Mo Temple
9 Pacific Place
10 Peak
11 St John's Cathedral
12 Western Market
13 Zoological and Botanical Gardens

Peak from the opposite shore as well as the panorama from The Peak itself.
The smaller IFC Tower 1, the luxurious Four Seasons Hotel and the IFC Shopping Mall are all part of the IFC complex. The INSIDER TIP rooftop garden on levels 3 and 4 between the towers is a must for all visitors – it has a wonderful view of the harbour and excellent restaurants! The complex is on reclaimed land created for the construction of the airport line railway station. *MTR Central*

4 FRENCH MISSION BUILDING

前法國外方傳道會大樓

(133 E3) (C12)

The most beautiful, and also largest, old building in the Central District was named after the French Mission that used it from 1915 to 1953. Today, the red-brick building with the white dome houses Hong Kong's Supreme Court of Appeal. It is not known exactly how old the building is, but it was already standing in 1880 before being

Place Shopping Centre. Hong Kong's most charming museum, the *Museum of Tea Ware* in the city's oldest colonial building *Flagstaff House*, shows all kinds of historical articles associated with tea and many other curios. In addition, large col-

Hong Kong Park: visitors' walkway in the treetops of the free-flight aviary

converted and extended to take on its present appearance in 1917. *Battery Path 炮台里 | above the old Bank of China | MTR Central*

▉5 HONG KONG PARK 香港公園 ★
(133 E3–4) *(ᗕ C–D 12–13)*

Visitors to Hong Kong's loveliest park can wander in the shade of old trees to the Tropics and Desert glasshouses, and go into a gigantic aviary with a zigzag walk through the treetops where 150 different species of Southeast Asian birds fly around over their heads. Newlyweds pose for photos near the registry office on the western edge of the 25 acre park. To the east, escalators glide up to the Pacific

our photos, historical illustrations and texts give an insight into the development of Chinese tea culture. The architecture of the *K.S. Lo Gallery* – a small collection of porcelain and seals provided by the donor Lo – only a few yards away, was adapted to match Flagstaff House. *Both museums Wed–Mon 10am–5pm | admission free | Cotton Tree Drive 紅棉路 | MTR Admiralty*

▉6 HSBC MAIN BUILDING 匯豐銀行總行大廈
(133 E3) *(ᗕ C12)*

The headquarters of Hong Kong's most important bank, the Hong Kong and Shanghai Banking Corporation, which is now only known under its acronym HSBC, is the most spectacular piece of architecture in Central. Although not particularly high, 179m (587)ft, the building that was designed by Norman Foster and first occupied in 1985, was the most expensive office building in the world at the time. The hi-tech construction is characterised by an unusual amount of architectural transparency. This can be seen in the open construction of load-bearing suspension trusses spanning 33m (108ft); this technique made it possible to keep almost the entire area of the ground floor open as a public space. Glass escalators lead up into the 52m (170ft)-high atrium that serves as a counter area; a glass false ceiling prevents the cooled air from escaping downwards; a computerised system of mirrors uses a light scoop on the south façade to draw daylight into the building from above. The only remnants of the former structure from 1935 are the two bronze lion guardians Stephen and Stitt. *Des Voeux Rd. Central* 德輔道中 | *MTR Central*

7 LEGCO BUILDING 立法會大樓
(133 E3) (𝑚 C11–12)

This building was erected between 1899 and 1910 to serve as the Supreme Court. Today, this is where the Legislative Council, Hong Kong's parliament meets. The gable of the west façade still has a statue of Justitia, blindfolded, with scales and a sword in her hands. The Legco Building is the only building remaining in Central to show a typical characteristic of Victorian architecture: a wide two-storey arcade of columns surrounds the building. Before the invention of air conditioning, this kept the interior cool and made it possible to leave the windows open during tropical downpours. *Statue Square* 皇后像廣場 | *MTR Central*

8 MAN MO TEMPLE 文武廟
(132 C2) (𝑚 B11)

This very popular temple complex in the antique dealers' district consists of three buildings. The *Main Hall* (left): Wen Chang, the god of literature (right) and General

RELAX & ENJOY

Podium Garden (131 D5–6) (𝑚 F9)
If you go over the wide bridge at the east end of the Avenue of Stars that leads to this square, a garden on the roof of the bus terminal, you can sit and relax under elegant awnings, and watch what's going on in the harbour without having to consume anything at all.

Iyara ● (133 D2) (𝑚 B11)
The second level of relaxation: here, next to the Central Escalator, you can have an affordable half-hour foot massage as well as – more expensive – beauty treatments or even a 4-hour

'Ultimate Half-day Escape'. *26 Cochrane St. | tel. 25 45 86 38 | www.iyarabeauty. com*

Spa in the Four Seasons Hotel (133 D2) (𝑚 C11)
The third level of relaxation: this 21,500ft² feel-good oasis in the luxury hotel in the IFC complex will make a dent in your budget but the list of treatments reads like pure poetry. There is no better way to be pampered. *8 Finance Street | reservation tel. 31 96 89 00 | www.fourseasons.com/ hongkong/spa*

Here, everything revolves around pious hopes: spirals of incense in the Man Mo Temple

Guan Yu the patron saint (right) sit, blackened by incense smoke, in magnificent vestments in the main shrine where they form the duo that gives the temple its name – the civil (Cantonese: *man*) and the military *(mo)*. The god of justice Bao Gong stands on the far left with his counterpart the god of the city on the extreme right. He informs the ten judges of hell – they can be seen on the left behind the entrance – about how the deceased had performed during their lifetime. The litters for carrying the gods, the dazzling brass articles – including two statues of deer as symbols of prosperity and longevity – and the carved altar are especially beautiful. Guan Yin is the main deity in the neighbouring *Lit Shing Kung*. An ancestral temple was set up in 1994: this is also where fortune tellers wait for their clients. A space for a 'spirit tablet' with the name of the deceased in the back room (hidden behind a transverse 'spirit wall') can cost as much as HK$180,000! Proceeds go to a hospital.

Daily 8am–6pm | 124 Hollywood Rd. 荷李活道 | MTR Sheung Wan

🟦9 PACIFIC PLACE 太古廣場
(133 F3–4) *(꿰 D12)*

This enormous complex fulfils many functions. It contains a cheerful shopping centre (with benches where you can sit without buying anything), restaurants (elegant in the eastern courtyard, inexpensive in the basement of the Seibu department store) and a cinema centre, while offices and four luxury hotels are located in the four towers that soar up above them. But possibly the most fascinating things are the escalators that glide up to Hong Kong Park from the western end. *Queensway 金鐘道 | MTR Admiralty*

🟦10 PEAK 山頂 ☀️
(132 A–C 3–5) *(꿰 A–B 12–13)*

This is the name of the whole area around the highest elevation on the island, 552m (1811ft) above sea level (132 B4) *(꿰 A12).*

In the 19th century, when tropical diseases were a problem in Hong Kong, the colonialists thought that The Peak was the only area on the island where one had a good chance of surviving the summer. Chinese were not permitted to live here until 1945. A trip in the old cable car, the Peak Tram, is an absolute must. You arrive at *Peak Tower* (132 C5) (*[] B13*) at the top, a complex of shops, restaurants, terraces and many other temptations.

It is a good idea however to ignore Peak Tower and turn right into Lugard Road after you leave the exit. Only people who take this 800 yard walk to the [INSIDER TIP] escarpment (132 B–C3) (*[] A12*) will experience the panorama in all its glory. The [INSIDER TIP] view at twilight is absolutely breathtaking. You will need around 50 minutes, without a break, for the entire ★ *Peak Trail* (no gradients). It is hardly worth climbing all the way to the top, but don't miss out on taking a break at the *Peak Lookout* (see: 'Food & Drink').

If you want a good walk, you should come back during the daytime and explore the amazing ⚊⚊ *Central Green Trail*. Go past Peak Tower towards the east *(Findlay Rd.)*. When you reach a junction, stay on the downhill side *(Severn Road)* until you reach *Hospital Path* (133 D5) (*[] C13*) signposted where you turn off to the left. When you reach the end, go a little way to the right. At the end of the car park you will see a sign with information on the trail that leads down along Chatham Path through subtropical vegetation – it frequently lightens to provide wonderful views of another jungle, the city's skyscrapers. Turn right where the trail intersects with another. The route crosses the Peak Tram track twice, goes down Clovelly Path, Brewin Park and Tramway Path until it ends at the lower terminal. *Duration: 1–1½ hours; be careful: the path is dangerously slippery when wet!*

● ⚊⚊ *Peak Tram*: Two air-conditioned carriages, each pulled by an almost 1500m (1mi)-long cable, run between the lower terminal on Garden Road (133 E3–4) (*[] C12*) and the top station at an altitude of 400m (1312ft) and overcome a difference in height of 367m (1200ft). There is absolutely no need to feel nervous; since it started operating in 1888 there has never been an accident.

▮▮ ST JOHN'S CATHEDRAL
聖約翰座堂 (133 E3) (*[] C12*)
The main Anglican church in Hong Kong was consecrated in 1849 and extended between 1869 and 1872. The Japanese occupying forces used the building as a casino in 1944/45 after which the interior decoration and windows had to be virtually completely renewed. Today, the Gothic Revival building almost disappears between all the skyscrapers. *Garden Rd.* 花園道 | *MTR Central*

12 WESTERN MARKET 西港城
(132 C2) (𝄞 B10–11)

This building, constructed in 1906, once housed a food market. After this moved to a larger, more modern site in 1988 (see Walk No. 3), the building was declared a historic monument. Cloth and souvenir dealers moved in. *Daily 10am–5pm | MTR Sheung Wan*

13 ZOOLOGICAL AND BOTANICAL GARDENS 動植物公園 ●
(133 D3–4) (𝄞 C12)

The garden is not very big but worth a visit. The scarlet ibises, flamingos and rare species of peacock are some of the main attractions. Visitors are also attracted by the orangutans and gibbons. The complex was founded in 1864 and a rest in the shade of the old trees is bliss. Early in the morning, many Hong Kongers come here to shadow box. *Daily 6am–10pm | admission free | Garden Rd.* 花園道 *| MTR Central*

WAN CHAI, CAUSEWAY BAY, HAPPY VALLEY

灣仔, 銅鑼灣, 跑馬地

Wan Chai, with its famous red-light district around Jaffe Road and Lockhart Road, in the centre of the north coast is a fine example of the give and take between old residential and new commercial buildings.

The *Convention and Exhibition Centre*, with its elegantly curved roof stretching out into the harbour, is the architectural highlight of this district. It is connected to two luxury hotels including the spectacular *Grand Hyatt* with the tower of the *Central Plaza* (134 A4) (𝄞 E12) soaring up behind

Sweeping elegance on the harbour in Wan Chai: the Convention and Exhibition Centre

SIGHTSEEING

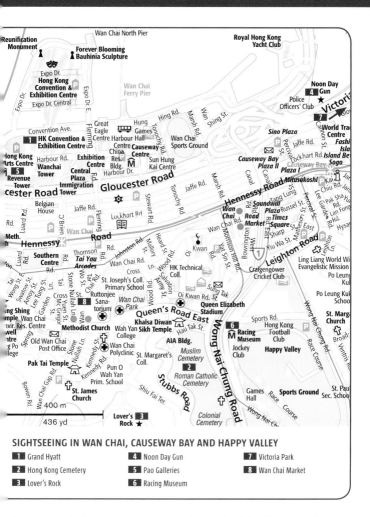

SIGHTSEEING IN WAN CHAI, CAUSEWAY BAY AND HAPPY VALLEY

- **1** Grand Hyatt
- **2** Hong Kong Cemetery
- **3** Lover's Rock
- **4** Noon Day Gun
- **5** Pao Galleries
- **6** Racing Museum
- **7** Victoria Park
- **8** Wan Chai Market

it. To the west, the *Academy for Performing Arts* and the *Arts Centre* have created two lively cultural centres *(134 A4) (ΜΠ E12)*. The oldest section of Wan Chai – south of Johnston Road, which used to be directly on the waterfront – is currently undergoing extensive redevelopment. Luckily, the picturesque *Wan Chai Market* has not been effected so far.

With its palatial shopping centres (including *Times Square* and the gigantic *Sogo* department store) *(134 C4) (ΜΠ G–H 11–12)*, cinemas, restaurants and a couple of pedestrian precincts, *Causeway Bay* to the east acts as one of the city's main recreational magnets and a paradise for shoppers. This is the place to get the real feel of Hong Kong especially in the evening.

If you need fresh air, you can find it in neighbouring Victoria Park.

Happy Valley further inland is dominated by Hong Kong's oldest racetrack. If you want to experience the Hong Kong passion for gambling at its best, don't miss out on a visit to the second racetrack in Sha Tin. The INSIDER TIP *Tourist Badge*, which you can purchase for HK$100 at the grand-stand entrance for Jockey Club members if you show your passport, will even make it possible to enter their elegant boxes (minimum age 18 years; please note: strict dress code! See *entertainment.hkjc.com/entertainment/English/tourist-corner*).

As is the case all over the north of the island, the tram is ideal for visitors who want to see what is going on. Some cars turn around at the corner of Victoria Park. More on trams under 'Central & Peak'.

Art Deco splendour in the foyer of the Grand Hyatt Hotel

▐1▐ GRAND HYATT 君悅酒店
(134 A3) (Ø E11–12)

Even after one-and-a-half centuries of British rule, 'understatement' is one word that has remained foreign in Hong Kong and the more than amply dimensioned Art Deco foyer in this hotel is one of the plushest examples of all. A golden oval sky hovers above an elegantly curved black marble staircase. *Harbour Rd. 港灣道 | MTR Wan Chai*

▐2▐ HONG KONG CEMETERY 香港墳場
(134 B–C 5–6) (Ø F13)

This colonial cemetery is Hong Kong's most historically important graveyard where not only British and Chinese, but also French, Germans and Russians have found their final resting places. *Tram to Happy Valley, entrance beneath the motorway approach to Aberdeen Tunnel*

▐3▐ INSIDER TIP LOVER'S ROCK
姻緣石 ☀ *(134 B5) (Ø E13)*

This 9m (30ft)-high, lavishly decorated monolith rises out of the jungle on a mountain slope above Wan Chai. Its phallic shape attracts women looking for Mr Right or hoping to have male children to come here and make sacrifices. The wonderful view and the hike along shady pedestrianised Bowen Road (with a keep-fit trail) are two other good reasons for a visit. *Above Bowen Rd. 寶雲道 to the east* of Wan Chai Gap Rd. | bus 15 from City Hall to Bowen Rd.

■4 NOON DAY GUN 午炮
(134 C3) (*ID G11*)

Every day in front of the Excelsior Hotel, at noon precisely, a shot is fired from the shining replica of a canon with which the Jardine trading house used to greet its ships coming into port from the shore. If you want to witness this charming little ceremony – a lovingly cultivated leftover from colonial days – take the tunnel beneath the urban motorway that starts next to the underground car park of the hotel at the World Trade Centre. *MTR Causeway Bay*

■5 PAO GALLERIES 包氏畫廊
(134 A4) (*ID E12*)

Changing contemporary exhibitions art are the order of the day here. *Daily 10am–* 8pm (closed during renovations) | entrance free | Arts Centre 香港藝術中心, 4th and 5th floor | 2 Harbour Rd. 港灣道

■6 RACING MUSEUM 賽馬博物館
(134 C5) (*ID F13*)

Documents, models, films and interactive monitors in the beautiful rooms with a panoramic view of the Happy Valley Racetrack give an impression of the history of horse racing in Hong Kong since its beginnings in 1846. *Tue–Sun 10am–5pm, 10am–9.30pm on race days | entrance free | Wong Nai Chung Rd. 黃泥涌道 | tel. information 2966 80 65 | 2/F, northern end of the grandstand building*

■7 VICTORIA PARK 維多利亞公園
(135 D3) (*ID G–H11*)

The 'green lung' of Causeway Bay was once an ocean inlet. It is an ideal place

KEEP FIT!

Bowen Road

Hong Kong's most beautiful jogging stretch: above Happy Valley and Wan Chai a traffic-free road takes you through leafy scenery – with occasional views of the forest of skyscrapers; keep-fit apparatus can also be found at various points on the route. Recommendation: go up over Wan Chai Gap **(134 A–B 5–6)** **(*ID E 13*)** and then run to the east to the end of Stubbs Road and, from there, take any bus back into town.

Victoria Park

This jogging track with keep-fit apparatus in the heart of the city also has a section where you can walk over loose round stones to massage your feet. **(135 D3)** **(*ID G–H11*)**

Hansen's Hikes and Rides

The Dane Michael Hansen offers regular hikes and bicycle tours in the New Territories. There is hardly a more pleasant way to stay fit and you will be able to discover the green side of Hong Kong at the same time. Information and reservations under: *www.hansens-hikes.com.*

Shadow boxing

Masters of Tai chi guan, the proper name of this form of Chinese gymnastics, go to the nearest park soon after 6am. Others gather in front of the *Museum of Art* **(130 C6)** **(*ID E9*)** on Mon, Wed, Thu and Fri at around 8am: that is where William and Pandora hold free training sessions commissioned by the HKTB.

for jogging or shadow boxing in the morning. The benches, footpaths and an area of gravel for foot massages are delightful at any time. *MTR Causeway Bay*

▇8 WAN CHAI MARKET 灣仔街市
(134 B4–5) *(⊠ E12)*
A colourful market, mainly selling all kinds of food, is held every day in the oldest residential area in Wan Chai – a perfect place to take in the atmosphere. *Tai Yuen Street* 太原街, *Cross Street* 交加街 *and neighbourhood | MTR Wan Chai*

The harbour promenade begins near the former railway station clock tower

WEST KOWLOON, TSIM SHA TSUI, YAU MA TEI

西九龍, 尖沙咀, 油麻地

Kowloon: 'Nine Dragons' is the name of the peninsula opposite the island – or more precisely, the area as far as Boundary Street (128–129 A–E5) *(⊠ D–G4)* **which formed the northern border of the Crown Colony after 1860.**

Today, Kowloon is considered to be the entire area south of the Lion Rock hills and consists of the southern section of the peninsula with two districts.
Tsim Sha Tsui: Tourism, with its hotels, bars and thousands of shops, is concentrated in the southernmost section of Kowloon. There is a never-ending row of shopping emporiums on the western shore from the *China Hong Kong City* (with its ferry terminal) (130 B–C5) *(⊠ D–E8)* to the *Ocean Terminal* (130 B6) *(⊠ D9)* where the cruise ships dock. At the southern tip, the *Clock Tower* rises up next to the Star Ferry landing stage – it is all that is left of the former railway station – with the *Cultural Centre* in a prime location behind it. The harbour promenade – as the *Avenue of Stars*, it pays homage to Hong Kong's most famous film actors and actresses – offers magnificent panoramic views. The main southwest axis of Kowloon, the more than 3.5km (2¼mi)-long *Nathan Road* (128 B5–6, 130 C1–6) *(⊠ E4–9)*, starts next to the time-honoured *Peninsula Hotel*. *Yau Ma Tei:* The top locations in this interesting district are the *Tin Hau Temple* with its shady forecourt, the *jade market* and

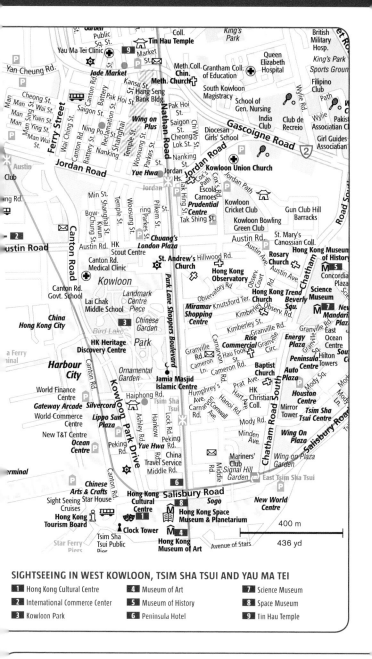

SIGHTSEEING IN WEST KOWLOON, TSIM SHA TSUI AND YAU MA TEI

1 Hong Kong Cultural Centre
2 International Commerce Center
3 Kowloon Park
4 Museum of Art
5 Museum of History
6 Peninsula Hotel
7 Science Museum
8 Space Museum
9 Tin Hau Temple

the *night market on Temple Street*; Walk No. 1 takes you to all of them.

You can shorten the distances between the various sights in Kowloon by taking the underground or one of the numerous buses that travel under and along Nathan Rd. Kowloon Park is a pleasant place to relax.

■1 HONG KONG CULTURAL CENTRE
香港文化中心 (130 C6) (*ጠ E9*)

The southern tip of Kowloon has been dominated by the salmon-pink tiled Cultural Centre since 1989. With its concert hall (2100 seats), a theatre (1750 seats), a studio theatre, a gigantic foyer and the Museum of Art, completed in 1991, it demonstrates the city's cultural ambitions. Many people made fun of the architecture (a 'ski slope') and it is strange – to put it mildly – that the almost windowless building completely ignores the exquisite view. *Salisbury Rd.* 梳士巴利道 *| MTR Tsim Sha Tsui*

■2 INTERNATIONAL COMMERCE CENTER 環球貿易廣場
(130 A–B4) (*ጠ C8*)

Hong Kong's new super skyscraper (484m/ 1588ft high) has been built at the entrance to the western harbour tunnel. The Ritz Carlton Hotel occupies 15 floors. The building also caters to the general public: ☼ INSIDERTIP *Sky 100*, at a height of 393m (1300ft,) has an observation platform with a panoramic view – and it is almost as high as The Peak *(daily 10am– 10pm, entrance fee HK$100). MTR Kowloon*

■3 KOWLOON PARK 九龍公園 ●
(130 C5) (*ጠ E8–9*)

The most interesting section of Kowloon's 'green lung' is the Sculpture Garden with contemporary works by local sculptors. Children will probably prefer the aviaries. There is also a swimming pool in the north of the park. The *Heritage Discovery Centre*

in the south holds exhibitions on Hong Kong's cultural heritage and also has a café. *Park daily 6.30am–midnight | Haiphong Rd.* 海防道 *| MTR Tsim Sha Tsui*

■4 MUSEUM OF ART 香港藝術館
★ ● (130 C6) (*ጠ E9*)

This building, opened in 1991 on the southern tip of Kowloon, does not seem very inviting at first sight but it is a demonstration of the cultural ambitions the city had at the time. Wealthy collectors donated a large number of masterpieces of classical Chinese art to the Museum. These mainly consisted of ink paintings and calligraphy, but also sculptures, lacquer ware, jade, bronzes, ceramics and textiles. Part of the 62,000ft² exhibition area is used to show interesting works of art by contemporary Hong Kong artists. *Fri–Wed 10am–6pm, Sat 10am–8pm | entrance fee HK$10, Wed free | Salisbury Rd.* 梳士巴利道 *| MTR Tsim Sha Tsui*

■5 MUSEUM OF HISTORY
香港歷史博物館 ★ ●
(131 D4) (*ጠ F8*)

This is one of the world's finest history museums. Visitors find it hard to tear themselves away from the great variety of subjects dealt with and the sophisticated presentation. Where the natural environment is explained, visitors see original-sized jungle trees and hear animals calling; in the cultural-history section, entire houses and theatre stages have been reconstructed, wall-sized photos of old Hong Kong merge with real objects on a scale of one-to-one – for example, a picture of the harbour blends in with a replica of a junk – and the historical chemist's shop even smells like one!

Interactive media, multilingual slide shows and historical film material make the journey through the past, known as 'The Hong Kong Story' complete. *Wed–Mon 10am–*

You will be able to admire Hong Kong's first commercial airliner in the Science Museum

6pm, Sun 10am–7pm | entrance fee HK$10, Wed free | 100 Chatham Road South | MTR Hung Hom

6 PENINSULA HOTEL 半島酒店
(130 C6) *(ⓜ E9)*

This almost overbearing hotel, which was extended with a skyscraper wing in 1996, is the most impressive architectural example of former colonial greatness. The opening of the hotel in 1928 was a milestone in Kowloon's development. In spite of the location in what was at the time an unattractive suburb, the hotel profited from the neighbouring railway station and the fantastic view of the island – although this is now obstructed. The best time to take in the atmosphere of the foyer with its magnificent golden plasterwork is at **INSIDER TIP** *high tea. Salisbury Rd.* 梳士巴利道 *| MTR Tsim Sha Tsui*

7 SCIENCE MUSEUM 香港科學館
(131 D4–5) *(ⓜ F8)*

The largest museum building in Hong Kong is devoted to science and technology. Many new educational ideas have been implemented here with great skill with most objects being hands-on exhibits. There is a room for special exhibitions on the ground floor and an introduction to the 'World of Mirrors'. The protection of the environment and endangered species, as well as life sciences, are dealt with on the next floor. There is also a *Children's Zone*. Children and teenagers will have a great time in the computer section on the first floor – where the entrance is located. One level up, communications, transport ('Betsy', Hong Kong's first commercial airliner, is a real eye-catcher on the ceiling), and food and household technology are dealt with. On the third floor is the energy efficiency display. The museum is particularly proud of its 20m (66ft)-high 'Energy Machine' in the atrium where rolling balls trigger all kinds of movements and sound effects. *Mon–Wed, Fri 1pm–9pm, Sat, Sun 10am–9pm | entrance fee HK$25, Wed free | 2 Science Museum Road* 科學館道 *| MTR Hung Hom*

■8 SPACE MUSEUM 香港太空館
(130 C6) (*♨ E9*)

This museum makes astronomy, solar engineering and space travel easy to understand and it will especially appeal to children and teenagers. The main attraction is the Planetarium. *Mon, Wed–Fri 1pm–9pm, Sat, Sun 10am–9pm | entrance fee HK$10, Wed free, Planetarium from HK$24 | Salisbury Rd. 梳士巴利道 | MTR Tsim Sha Tsui*

■9 TIN HAU TEMPLE 天后廟
(130 C3) (*♨ E7*)

Tin Hau, the patron saint of seafarers, should have an open view of the ocean so that she can tell when there are problems at sea – but the skyscrapers ruin any chance of her being able to see this from the large Tin Hau temple in Yau Ma Tai. The statue of the goddess is in the central hall of a series of five temple buildings where many other deities are also worshipped. Guan Yin (Bodhisattva of Compassion), the main figure in the temple hall to the south, is positioned to the right of the principal goddess. Paper gifts for the dead, waiting to be burned in one of the ovens between the buildings and sent to the hereafter, are left in the temple on the north side. *Daily 8am–5pm | Public Square St. 眾坊街 | MTR Yau Ma Tei*

MONG KOK

旺角

⭐ **This extremely densely populated district of the city delights its visitors with its large variety of street markets and other shopping possibilities.**

Some sections of the streets in Mong Kok have even been turned into pedestrian precincts – something very rare in Hong Kong. The markets for food, flowers and birds are described below; see 'Shopping' for information on the market on Fa Yuen Street and the Ladies' Market.

An idyllic spot in the big city: the bird market in Mong Kok

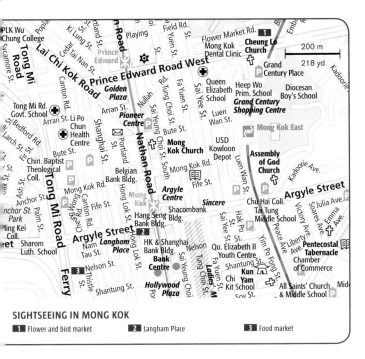

SIGHTSEEING IN MONG KOK

■1 Flower and bird market ■2 Langham Place ■3 Food market

The market where ornamental fish are sold on *Tung Choi Street* near Bute Street (128 B6) (*∅ D–E5*) is an attractive place to go for a stroll and get a glimpse of everyday life.

■1 FLOWER AND BIRD MARKET
花墟, 園圃街雀鳥花園
(128 B–C5) (*∅ E4*)

These are actually two separate markets but you have to pass the flower market on your way to the bird market. The Yuen Po Street Bird Garden, to give it its proper name, was specifically established here – with small houses and a lot of green, it is an idyllic, photogenic location and it is closed to traffic! The flower market is more or less just a block of houses (on the south side of Flower Market Road) with countless flower and plant shops. *MTR Prince Edward*

■2 LANGHAM PLACE 朗豪坊
(130 C1) (*∅ E5*)

Its architecture makes Hong Kong's futuristic shoppers' paradise the most spectacular of all – 9 storeys high, with a winter garden glazed on two sides and no right angles. *Portland Street/corner of Argyle Street* 砵蘭街/亞皆老街 | *MTR Mong Kok*

■3 FOOD MARKET 旺角街市
(130 B1) (*∅ D5*)

All the ingredients needed for Cantonese cooking are sold every day on the corner of Argyle Street and Canton Road and in interesting Nelson Street. Vegetables and dried mushrooms, fruit and meat, as well as fish, mussels, toads and crabs that are all still alive. The market is at its liveliest in the morning. *MTR Mong Kok*

MORE SIGHTS

ABERDEEN 香港仔
(136 A–C 2–4) (*B–D 16–17*)

This skyscraper settlement in the south-west of the island is still described as a 'fishing village' in some brochures and catalogues – what a misrepresentation!

to Ap Lei Chau opposite the exclusive Yacht Club. It serves good dim sums. If you feel like taking a sampan trip, bargain with the ladies who approach you on the promenade with their cries of 'Sampan, sampan!' (around HK$60 per person for 30 minutes). *Bus 70 from Exchange Square to the terminus, then to the west and cross over the pedestrian bridge; the ferries to the restaurant leave from the promenade a few yards to the right.*

Full steam ahead: sampan tours are the hit in the harbour at Aberdeen

Harbour: The formerly famous junk town no longer looks like it did in countless films. Nobody lives permanently on the water here anymore but the more than 100 motorised junks remaining at least create a touch of the exotic atmosphere of the Far East. The free ferry trip to the gigantic floating restaurant *Jumbo* will give you some idea of this. This monument to Chinese kitsch, laden down with gold, is anchored on the other side of the bridge

Cemetery: Ancestors deserve the very best to make sure that they bestow their blessings on the living which is why Cantonese graves always enjoy prime locations – although they usually get built up after a while in Hong Kong. The large *Aberdeen Chinese Permanent Cemetery* is probably the closest you will come to experiencing the original. A visit is especially worthwhile at the Ching Ming and 'double nine' – held on the 9 day of the

9 month in the Chinese calendar – festivals when offerings are made at the graves. Entrance over a flight of steps on the slope. *(136 A2–3) (∅ B16–17)*

CHI LIN NUNNERY ●
志蓮淨苑 *(U D1) (∅ 0)*

The newest of Hong Kong's temple convents was completed in 2000. It is also the most representative because it was built as a classical Chinese wooden construction in the massive, but simple style of the Tang period. The mostly gilded pictures show that it is still possible to create impressive Buddhist works of art. *Daily 9am–4.30pm*

Visitors reach the superbly cultivated *Nan Lian Garden (daily 7am–9pm | entrance free | www.nanliangarden.org)* opposite the convent over a bridge. The 9 acres make it the largest example of Chinese garden art in Hong Kong. It also has an exquisite vegetarian restaurant. *At the east end of Fung Tak Rd. 鳳德道 | MTR Diamond Hill, exit C2*

LION ROCK 獅子山 *(139 D3) (∅ 0)*

This conspicuous 495m (1624ft)-high peak in the shape of a lion's head is more of an eyecatcher than a hiking destination. It gave its name to the entire range of hills that borders Kowloon to the north.

OCEAN PARK 海洋公園 ★ ☼
(137 E–F 3–4, D–E 5–6) (∅ E–F 17–20)

Hong Kong's most delightful leisure park is a mixture of an amusement park, zoo and circus in a fantastic location with a view over the South China Sea. The 217-acre complex is divided into two sections: *Waterfront* near the entrance and *Summit* higher up. The two are connected by a 1.5km (1mi) cable railway as well as the *Ocean Express*, an underground cable car that simulates an underwater voyage. Maritime themes set the tone, but the range of attractions is much wider. *Waterfront* is more for young visitors with children's merry-go-rounds, games of skill and trained sea lions – this is also where Hong Kong's four panda bears are at home, and

BOOKS & FILMS

▶ **Noble House** – Written by James Clavell, probably the most famous novel about Hong Kong deals with intrigues for economic power (1981)

▶ **Chungking Express** – A genuine Hong Kong film that made it into the cinemas of the west. It tells two love stories set in the city's police milieu (1994, directed by Wong Kar Wei).

▶ **Love is a Many-Splendored Thing** – The western/oriental love story by Han Suyin (1952) is set in the difficult post-war years in Hong Kong.

▶ **The World of Suzie Wong** – Richard Mason wrote the book about the beauty from the Wan Chai red-light district who became world famous through the film adaptation with William Holden and Nancy Kwan (1960, directed by Richard Quine).

▶ **The Man with the Golden Gun** – Hong Kong is the favourite location for showing the exotic east in western films. Chinese play only supporting roles and it is the same in this James Bond film with Roger Moore (1974, directed by Guy Hamilton).

South-East Asian birds and otters live in a free flight hall. The *Aqua City*, an aquarium 3-floors deep with 5000 fish of 400 species, is the pride of the park. Ocean Park is also involved in protecting endangered species; part of the proceeds flow into a foundation.

your-visit/calendar | Bus 629 from MTR Admiralty, exit B

REPULSE BAY 淺水灣 ● (U D5) (*[1] 0*)
Hong Kong's most popular beach for swimming is always overcrowded during the summer months. Swimming out to one

Suitable environment: Murray House in Stanley is the home of the Maritime Museum

Visitors learn to about nature in the *Summit* region too, where there is a magnificent **INSIDER TIP** jellyfish aquarium and an open-air enclosure in the form of an artificial rocky coast for seals, complete with waves, at *Pacific Pier*. A looping track and other rides provide plenty of thrills nearby. Escalators glide down to the lower level with the *Raging River* rapids ride. *Mon–Sat 10am–7.30pm, Sun 9.30am–7.30pm | entrance fee HK$250 | for information on possible changes and performance times, see www.oceanpark.com.hk/html/en/plan-*

of the pontoons and being gently rocked by the waves is a wonderful way to relax. There are many restaurants and a wonderfully kitschy Tin Hau temple at the southern end.

STANLEY 赤柱 ★ (U D6) (*[1] 0*)
Stanley is Hong Kong's southernmost area. Most visitors go to the large clothes market in the centre. Other attractions include the Promenade with *Murray House* that was originally built in 1844 and was to be demolished for the construction of the Bank

of China Tower in 1982. It was moved here and now houses the *Maritime Museum*: models, original ship parts, reproductions and audiovisual media document seafaring in the Far East, as well as life in Hong Kong's harbour in the 20th century. *Museum Tue–Sun 10am–6pm | entrance fee HK$20 | www.hkmaritimemuseum.org | Buses 6, 6X from Exchange Square*

VICTORIA HARBOUR 維多利亞港
(U C3) (*ɒ A–H 6–11*)
This is really the heart of Hong Kong and one of world's largest container ports. Kwai Chung in the northwest of Kowloon is the loading centre. The *Star Ferry Company* and *Watertours* organise daily tours.

WONG TAI SIN TEMPLE
黃大仙祠 ★ ● (129 F2) (*ɒ H1–2*)
Every year more than 3 million faithful make offerings to a miracle-working saint here. The complex also has a 2-storey building with rooms for 160 fortune tellers and a shop selling devotional objects. The main hall with its double roof – closed to the public – was consecrated in 1973, most of the others in 1982. This is where you will be able to experience Hong Kong's syncretism; Confucius, Lao Tse and Buddha are also worshipped here. A clinic is part of the temple complex; it belongs to the Sik Sik Yuen charity organisation and is financed through donations made by the faithful. *Daily 7am–5.30pm | MTR Wong Tai Sin, exits A and B*

FURTHER AFIELD

CHEUNG CHAU 長洲
(138 B–C5) (*ɒ 0*)
Translated, Cheung Chau means 'Long Land' and it is the largest and liveliest of all the traditional settlements in Hong Kong. The narrow streets are lined with 2-storey houses clustered together. With the exception of a few mini-pickups, there are no cars. There are still some junks in the harbour although there has been a great decline in fishing. The quay is lined with fish restaurants and kiosks where holiday flats can be booked; it is also possible to rent bikes.

If you turn to the left coming from the landing place, you reach a large square (with a sports ground in front of it) with the religious centre of the community, the *Pak Tai Temple* from 1783, where the patron saint, the Emperor of the Northern Heaven, is honoured. He is thanked every year during the famous Buns Festival. You can then head south (parallel to the quay) along narrow Pak She Street with many small shops.

Turn to the left when you come to the former market square (Tung Wan Road) and walk past a revered tree until you reach the outskirts of the settlement. There is a prehistoric scratch drawing preserved on a rock ledge below the Warwick Hotel at the southern end. It is the most accessible example of this type of rock picture in the Hong Kong territory; most of them were discovered near the shore in recent decades. Nothing is known about their age or who drew them (probably not Chinese) and they show animal forms stylised to geometrical patterns.

Go up Cheung Chau Sports Road above the hotel and take Fa Peng Road to Peak Road and turn left. Follow this about 2.2km (1½mi) to the west to *Care Village* in the southwest and take the sampan ferry from there back to the main settlement. If you also intend to go swimming, half a day will not be enough for Cheung Chau and a full day is never too long. *Ferries from Central, Pier 5, approx. twice an hour, travelling time 60 mins (30, by express ferry)*

FURTHER AFIELD

AIRPORT 國際機場 AND
TSING MA BRIDGE 青馬大橋

Gigantic is simply not the right word. The artificial island that was created to take the place of Chek Lap Kok isle for the airport (138 A4) (*ØØ O*) is the same size as Kowloon. The terminal building is 1.27km (more than ¾mi) long.

The transport links demanded the utmost skill on the part of the engineers. The ten individual projects include the western six-lane harbour tunnel and the largest road-rail suspension bridge in the world, the Tsing Ma Bridge (138 C3) (*ØØ O*). With its span of 1377m (4518ft) it is even longer than the Golden Gate Bridge in San Francisco.

Visitors get a fine panoramic view of the construction and its creation in the ⚜ *Lantau Link Visitors Centre | Mon–Fri 10am–5pm, Sat, Sun 10am–6.30pm | at the eastern end of the bridge | minibus 308M from MTR Tsing Yi, exit A1 on level 1 (Mon–Fri hourly10am–4pm, Sat, Sun 9.30am–6.30pm)*.

LAMMA ISLAND 南丫島
(138–139 C–D5) (*ØØ O*)

Beaches, hills and fish restaurants: Hong Kong's third largest island. Lamma, as well as all the other small islands, is car-free. Day-trippers come for a swim – there are two pleasant beaches on the island: *Hung Shing Yeh* in the north and INSIDERTIP *Lo So Shing* in the centre – and to eat. There is a row of fish restaurants along the harbour front in the village of Sok Kwu Wan; the best is the *Rainbow (Moderate)*. You can rent rooms in Yung Shue Wan, the peaceful second village. Here, you can also enjoy your meal on a terrace near the water. It will take you around 90 minutes to walk across reforested hills from one village to the next. *Ferries from Central, Pier 4, every half to two hours, travelling time 30–50 mins.*

LANTAU 大嶼山 AND
PO LIN MONASTERY 寶蓮寺 ★
(138 A–B 4–5) (*ØØ O*)

You should explore Hong Kong's largest island Lantau by bus or taxi; there are enough attractions for a full day. A new era opened up for Lantau when the airport was built; with it, came new roads and railway tracks, followed by a satellite city and, in 2005, Disneyland. However, parts of the islands have remained almost deserted.

Hong Kong's largest religious building, *Po Lin Monastery*, is located at an altitude of 460m (1500ft) on the Ngong Ping Plateau. The Buddhist 'Monastery of the Precious Lotus' was consecrated in 1927 and the main hall, inspired by Peking's palace architecture, in 1970. The monastery has prospered as a destination for outings.

Visitors, including many from foreign countries, have streamed to the monastery since the world's largest open-air bronze Buddha (22m/72ft high, 34m/112ft with the stone base) was erected there in 1993. In 2006, *Ngong Ping 360* started operating. This includes a 5.7km (3½mi)-long cable car (travelling time: 25 min. from the MTR terminus Tung Chung to the Buddha) as well as Ngong Ping Village at the top with shops, restaurants and a multimedia show 'Walking with Buddha' that describes the life of Gautama Buddha. Take the cable car up and walk or take the bus down.

The fishing village *Tai O* at the western end of the island mainly consists of wooden houses covered with sheet metal on stilts that appear to hover over the surface of the water. The strange mudskipper fish jump around and mangroves grow in some places. Lantau's loveliest beaches *Pui O* and *Cheung Sha* are at the centre of the south coast. Some forts from the 17th century, built to protect the area from pirates, are historically important; the largest can be visited at the southern end of *Tung Chung*.

The 70km (43½mi) *Lantau Trail* starts at Mui Wo in the northeast and leads, in twelve stages, over the hills to the south-

taurants and fishmongers selling the greatest variety of seafood available anywhere in Hong Kong. Many of the houses float above the water on stilts. Follow the double-bend to the right and then left

By sampan through the fishing village of Tai O on the west of Lantau Island

west cape and back again along the coast. The third stage is spectacular but quite steep; it goes over the barren *Lantau Peak* (934m/3064ft) to Po Lin Monastery. Easier routes: from the monastery to the south through the forest to the road or to the northeast as far as Tung Chung (Fort, underground). *Ferries from Central, Pier 6, to Mui Wo every 30–50 mins., travelling time 1 hour; from Mui Wo with bus no. 2 to Ngong Ping (monastery), with no. 1 to Tai O and with 3M to Tung Chung; also MTR Tung Chung*

INSIDER TIP LEI YUE MUN 鯉魚門
(U E3) (*◎ 0*)
A stroll through a village that is easy to reach. The fishing settlement of Lei Yue Mun more or less only consists of one single long street. It is lined with fish res-

and after about 500m you will reach some large rocks and the village temple in honour of the 'Empress of Heaven' Tin Hau. *MTR Kwun Tong line or Tseung Kwan O line to Yan Tong, exit A2, then walk 600m; the village begins at the junk port.*

INSIDER TIP MAI PO NATURE RESERVE
米埔 ⓒ (138 B–C 1–2) (*◎ 0*)
The fish and shrimp pools, mud flats and Hong Kong's last large belt of mangroves in the Mai Po Nature Reserve in the amphibian northwest of the New Territories provide plenty of nourishment and shelter for silver herons, ibises, kingfishers and another 250 species of birds. Many migratory birds spend the winter here. The World Wide Fund for Nature (WWF) has established an information centre and observation sites in the reserve. Visits only as part

of a guided tour. *Only Sat, Sun | WWH: 1 Tramway Path | tel. 25 26 10 11 | www.wwf. org.hk/en/getinvolved/gomaipo*

NEW TERRITORIES 新界

Although they actually include all the areas that are not part of Kowloon or Hong Kong Island, people think of them as the mainland beyond the range of hills that forms the boundary to the north and east of Kowloon. This is the site of gigantic satellite towns as well as still virtually impassable terrain with Hong Kong's highest elevation *Tai Mo Shan* (957m/3140ft). Two excellent tours give a fine overview of the main sights *(duration around 5 hours each, HK$380)*; they can booked at *Gray Line Tours (tel. 23 68 71 11 | www.grayline. com.hk)*. The 'Heritage Tour' includes a visit to an old clan village, typical of how the New Territories used to be, complete with ancestral temple, to the residence of an imperial official, to the market temple in *Tai Po* and the trees that are worshiped as being holy. 'Land Between' offers a colourful selection with a temple monastery, the heron reserve *Luk Keng* and fish farms. You will see a great deal of the landscape, as well as two or three satellite towns, on both tours.

Amah Rock (139 D3) *(ω O)*: Once upon a time a fisherman failed to return from sea. Every day, his faithful wife – with their child in a baby sling – climbed up the mountain to watch out for a sign of him. Finally, the gods took mercy on her and she was reunited with the drowned man. Amah Rock is a sign of her fidelity. You have an especially good view of it from the train line near Tai Wai.

Mountain hiking: The *MacLehose Trail*, named after a former governor, runs from east to west over 100km (62mi) divided into 10 stages. The most picturesque sections (stages 1 and 2) takes hikers along the Sai Kung Peninsula. The 75km (47mi) *Wilson Trail* crosses the New Territories from north to south.

GAMBLING FEVER & RUGBY

▶ *Horse racing in Hong Kong:* Races have been held in *Happy Valley* (134 C5) *(ω F–G13)* since 1846 and now usually take place on Wed evening. The *Sha Tim* (139 D3) *(ω O)* track was added in 1978: it is used at weekends. On average, almost 50,000 spectators come to each event. The racing season lasts from Sept to early June. *www.hkjc.com/ english/index.asp.*

▶ *Horse racing in Macau:* The *Taipa* racetrack, opened in 1991, holds 15,000 spectators. Most races take place at weekends. Entrance to the lower levels is free. *Tel. 28 82 08 68* (146 A–B2) *(ω a–b8)*

▶ *Dog races:* A Macau speciality. Fifteen races are held on Saturdays and Sundays starting at 7.30pm. *Canídromo | Avenida General Castelo Branco | tel. 28 33 33 99* (144 C–D2) *(ω c–d2)*

▶ *Rugby:* Another popular sport. The highlight every year is the *Hong Kong Sevens (www.hksevens.com)*, an international competition held in the Hong Kong Stadium (135 D5) *(ω H13)* at the end of March.

SAI KUNG PENINSULA 西貢半島 AND TAP MUN 塔門 (139 E–F 2–3) (*ØØ 0*)

The rugged, almost deserted peninsula lies far to the east and is the best destination for a not-too-strenuous day-long walk. Take the 8.30am ferry from Ma Liu Shui Pier (139 D2–3) (*ØØ 0*) *(MTR University Station, exit B, walk to the left and follow the signs to 'Pier' or 'Landing Steps').* The sea journey takes you along the mountainous shore of Tolo Harbour to *Tap Mun Island* with its old fishing and farming village. You can spend an hour there until the ferry comes back for the return journey or travel two stations further to *Chek Keng* and take the trail over the saddle of the mountain to the southeast. The reward for the 3.5km (2¼mi) walk is **INSIDER TIP** *Tai Long Wan* the 'Bay of Big Waves' with Hong Kong's two most fabulous beaches; there are simple restaurants in the nearby village.

Then it's back to Chek Keng; this time not to the pier but to the left and another 3.5km (2¼mi) to the next bay *Wong Shek*. A bus to **INSIDER TIP** *Sai Kung*, the starting point for picturesque boat trips through the labyrinth of islands in Port Shelter and Rocky Harbour, departs from Wong Shek every 30 mins. During the week, you can take a 45-min. sampan cruise around *Sharp Island* (Kiu Tsui Chau) for as little as HK$150. There is also a row of fish restaurants at the harbour. *Return by bus 92 to MTR Diamond Hill*

SHA TIN 沙田 (139 D3) (*ØØ 0*)

There are two interesting destinations near the train station in this gigantic satellite town. In addition to temporary exhibitions, the *Heritage Museum* has a fantastic section devoted to the history and culture of the New Territories. *From the station (exit A, then to the right, down the escalator) through the bus station and follow the road on the right; around 10 mins.*

Excursion to Sha Tin: pagoda in the Temple of the 10,000 Buddhas

The *Temple of 10,000 Buddhas* has occupied its site in the mountains since 1957. The path through the wood is lined with life-sized figures – some of them, gold-plated – of the 500 Luohan (Buddhist monks). The interior walls of the main hall are covered with shelves with 12,800 small gilded statues of Buddha. There are many other figures, usually brightly coloured, in the forecourt, as well as a pagoda. *Cross the railway, follow the street on the right past the Grand Central Plaza skyscraper complex, turn left onto Pak Tau Street, then right to Sheung Wo Che Street and follow the footpath up the valley*

FOOD & DRINK

Hong Kong is a paradise for gourmets where going out to eat is part of everyday life.

And that has led to an opulent range of restaurants ranging from those for ordinary people to extremely elegant, from Chinese to European.

CHINESE CUISINE

Most Hong Kongers are Cantonese and their cooking is unquestionably the queen of all regional cuisines of China. Backbiters from other parts of the country say that the Cantonese would eat anything on four legs except a table and everything that swims, with the exception of ships, and –

as long is it wasn't a plane – anything that flies. And, admittedly, chickens' feet and jellyfish might not be everyone's favourite titbit. But, the Cantonese mastery in using even the most unusual ingredients has led to the fascinating variety of dishes and Hong Kong's cooks are continuously adding new creations.

First and foremost – everything has to be fresh! Chickens are usually only slaughtered after they have been bought; seafood swims in an aquarium or pond until guests orders it. This is to ensure that the natural flavours can be experienced to the full. And is also the result of the way food is cooked – rapid searing or

Photo: Dim sums

Gourmet restaurants and cookhouses: every day you will be able to experience new culinary highlights – and not only Chinese cuisine

steaming – and a reasonable, even frugal, use of spices.

What should you order? Of course, seafood is the first choice. Pork and chicken are always good too. Roast duck is another delicious dish; you dunk it in plum sauce. There are also excellent vegetarian dishes which frequently offer amazing imitations of meat and fish for those who prefer to let animals stay alive.

However, the *dim sums* are the real highlight. It is not actually a dish but the edible part of *yam cha*, Cantonese tea culture. Small delicacies are served along with tea in the teahouses and restaurants from early in the morning to the afternoon – small dumplings filled with shrimps or shark meat, ribs in plum sauce, fried balls filled with lotus-seed paste and dozens of other kinds of 'heart's delights' – which is what dim sum means. In some restaurants, buffet trolleys are pushed through the rows of tables; in others, guests order by marking their choice on special order forms. Very few experiences in Hong Kong are more

from Chaozhou are not to be overlooked. Birds' nests are famous – but very expensive. Another thing you will not forget is the strong, bitter Chaozhou digestive tea that is drunk out of tiny cups.

A Chinese meal – the more diners, the greater the variety of dishes

impressive and authentic than going to a INSIDER TIP Sunday lunchtime *yam cha* (tea drinking session) when whole families descend on the – often gigantic and lavishly decorated – teahouses where the noise they make brings the roof down. The other regional cuisines of China also profit from the great variety of excellent products and high culinary standard of Hong Kong and often taste at least as good here as they do in their region of origin: Peking cooking is famous for the Peking Duck, fire pot and noodle dishes, East Chinese cooking from Shanghai and Hangzhou prefers more substantial food (sometime flavoured with tea leaves), while extremely spicy dishes are typical of Szechuan cuisine. And the hearty dishes

You should be in a group to really enjoy a meal in a Chinese restaurant. The number of delights increases with the number of diners, nobody just orders 'his or her' meal, everybody shares everything on the table. One person takes charge of ordering. Usually, one more dish than the number of guests is ordered and a selection is made from the various categories – duck, chicken, pork, shrimps, fish and so on – as well as a soup. The huge choice of seafood makes it possible for you to put together a purely maritime meal.

Most of the better restaurants have an English menu and you will often find a waiter who can help you in others – if they are not too busy. It is a good idea to book in advance in most restaurants.

DRINKS

Tea is the perfect beverage to accompany a Cantonese meal – especially the non-fermented green or semi-fermented Wulong tea (leaves are brewed twice). There is usually only a limited choice of wine in Chinese restaurants. Beer is a better idea, especially to go with the heavier dishes from other regions. Freshly-pressed fruit juices from booths as well as soya milk (sold as 'Vitasoy') are ideal refreshments when out and about.

NON-CHINESE COOKING

The cuisine of other countries plays a major role in Hong Kong's culinary variety. Curry fans will find what they are looking for in the Indian and Indonesian restaurants, aficionados of pepper and chilli will feel at home with the Koreans and Thais (wash it down with beer), and lovers of fresh products and raw fish can choose from the many Japanese restaurants. You also do not have to do without European cooking but the prices are often similar to those in expensive restaurants at home. Eating in a European restaurant in Hong Kong is not only something those suffering from homesickness do; many chefs have been inspired by the wealth of different local products and cooking techniques.

BREAKFAST

The breakfast served in large hotels is first-rate but unreasonably expensive. A more economical alternative is to have café au lait, croissants, etc. in one of the branches of *Délifrance*, e.g. 45–51 Chatham Road South (131 D5) (*ん F9*) or 1/F Worldwide Plaza, Pedder Street (133 D–E3) (*ん C11*). If you need a cup of tea to get you going in the morning, you should start your day with dim sums in a teahouse, e.g. from 7.30am at *Causeway Plaza II | Percival St., corner Lockhart Rd. (entrance Lockhart Rd.)* (134 C4) (*ん G12*).

SWEETS

Some special restaurants are devoted entirely to sweet temptations; one is *Hui Lau Shan Healthy Dessert | Sai Yeung Choi St. South 58–60* (130 C1) (*ん E5*), *24–30 Percival St.* (134 C3–4) (*ん G12*), and at other locations.

The prices are for à la carte meals, without expensive specialities such as abalone and swallows' nests.

BISTRO MANCHU 滿漢居
(133 D3) (*ん B11*)
This cheerful little restaurant serves cooking from Northern China including Jiaozi

---

MARCO POLO HIGHLIGHTS

⭐ **Chuen Kee**
Seafood fresh from the pool with a view of the harbour and a glass of wine → p. 58

⭐ **Din Tai Fung**
The dumpling king: not very cosy, but oh so good! → p. 59

⭐ **Hunan Garden**
Live music to go with a fine meal in the heart of the financial district → p. 59

⭐ **Yung Kee**
The epitome of culinary excellence in Hong Kong → p. 61

⭐ **Indochine 1929**
Vietnamese nostalgia: the best of three worlds → p. 62

⭐ **Peak Lookout**
Hong Kong's most beautiful restaurant → p. 63

CHINESE CUISINE

dumplings Peking style and various sweet-and-sour dishes. *33 Elgin St. 伊利近街 | tel. 25 36 92 18 | Budget*

CHUEN KEE 全記海鮮菜館 ★
(139 E3) (*∅ 0*)

Fish and seafood fresh from the pool. You can even sit outside and watch the boats bobbing up and down in the harbour. The restaurant caters to foreign guests and has a supply of cooled white wine. *Sai Kung | 53 Hoi Pong St. 海傍街 | Harbour Promenade, south end beyond the ceremonial gate | tel. 27 911 95 | bus 92 from MTR Diamond Hill | Moderate–Expensive*

CRYSTAL JADE 翡翠拉麵小籠包
(130 B–C5) (*∅ D–E9*)

If you are lucky, you might be able to enjoy traditional Shanghai cooking with a view of the harbour here. There are delicious dumplings and the servings of noodles are more than satisfying. You can pass the time waiting for a free table – you are given a number – window shopping. *Shop 3328, Gateway Arcade Harbour City 海港城港威商場 | tel. 26 22 26 99 | other branches | Budget*

INSIDER TIP ▶ DIM SUM 譽滿坊 ●
(135 D6) (*∅ G14*)

The name tells you what you will be served but not how good they are, that you can order from an English menu with photographs, and just how charming the nostalgic atmosphere created by the wood, fans and old posters is in this 14-table teahouse. Especially typical at lunchtime (and cheaper than in the evening); you will probably have a long wait on Sunday! *63 Sing Woo Rd. 成和道 | tel. 28 34 88 93 | Budget–Moderate*

GOURMET RESTAURANTS

Bo Innovation 廚魔
(134 A4) (*∅ E12*)

Molecular cooking in Chinese. Some people find it too experimental but you can be sure of entering new culinary territory. The 'Wall Street Journal' even wrote an article about it when it opened. From HK$750. *18 Ship St. 船街 (Lift) | tel. 28 50 83 71 | www.boinnovation.com*

Caprice ✷ (133 D2) (*∅ C11*)

The French haute cuisine in the culinary flagship Four Season's Hotel vies with the view of the open kitchen and the panorama of Victoria Harbour. 3 Michelin stars. From HK$1000. *3 Finance St. 金融街 | tel. 31 96 88 60*

Forum (134 C4) (*∅ G12*)

Cantonese. Chef Yeung Kwun Yat is considered the world's greatest abalone expert and here the top quality can reach astronomical prices of up to HK$20,000 each. If you are a little more modest, you might be able to get away with around HK$750 per person. *485 Lockhart Rd. 駱克道 | tel. 28 91 25 55*

Pierre (133 E3) (*∅ C11*)

Pierre Gagnaire, the master chef who gave his name to this restaurant, shows how it's done: modern, but hearty and light French cuisine. Large windows with views of Hong Kong's harbour and inner city. From HK$1000. *25/F, Mandarin Oriental | 5 Connaught Rd. Central 干諾道中 | tel. 28 25 40 01*

DIN TAI FUNG 鼎泰豐 ★

You will almost certainly have to queue up for a while if you want to enjoy the delicious dumplings and other small dishes from Shanghai and Taiwan served here. There is even a card giving instructions on how to eat the famous, delicate *xiaolongbao* that not only contain a solid filling but also hot broth. *68 Yee Wo St. 怡和街 | tel. 31 60 89 98 (135 D4) (Ⓜ G12); 3/F, 30 Canton Rd. 廣東道 | tel. 27 30 69 28 (130 C5) (Ⓜ E9) | Budget*

HUNAN GARDEN 洞庭樓 ★
(133 D–E2) (Ⓜ C11)

Hunan cuisine is usually very spicy but this restaurant shows mercy and notes just how hot the individual dishes really are on the menu. The prices are just as comforting in spite of the location near the Stock Exchange. Classical Chinese music is played in the evening – live. *Forum | Exchange Square 交易廣場富臨閣 | tel. 28 68 28 80 | Moderate*

INSIDER TIP KUNG TAK LAM
功德林 😊 🕭 (130 C5) (Ⓜ E9)

Vegetarian Shanghai cuisine in a modern environment with a view of the harbour. The organic ingredients come from the restaurant's own garden. An ideal place for dim sums at lunchtime. *1 Peking Rd. 北京道, 7th floor | tel. 23 12 78 00 | Budget*

INSIDER TIP LUK YU 陸羽茶室
(133 D3) (Ⓜ C11)

Cantonese. The multi-storey restaurant, named after the patron saint of tea, opened in 1933 and, with its original decoration and stern waiters who are almost as old, is a living monument. It is best in the morning or at lunchtime for tea and dim sums. *24–26 Stanley St. 士丹利街 | tel. 25 23 54 64 | morning (from 7am) and lunch with dim sums: Moderate, at other times: Expensive*

MAXIM'S PALACE 美心皇宮 ●
(133 E3) (Ⓜ D11)

The fact that the view of the harbour is now usually one of building sites has not

Dim sum – the highlight of Cantonese cuisine

LOCAL SPECIALITIES

DIM SUM

Most dim sum menus are only in Chinese but you will often find a waiter or waitress who can help you with your order.

CHINESE MEALS & INGREDIENTS

▶ **Abalone** – meat of a sea snail, fresh or dried
▶ **Beggar's chicken** – A whole chicken is coated with clay and then roasted in its own juices
▶ **Bird's nest** – Swallows' nests served as a soup or dessert
▶ **Congee** – Rice soup, either plain or with vegetables or meat
▶ **Double sautéed pork** – pork, cooked twice
▶ **Fish balls** – Fish and shrimp meat rolled into balls and served in broth
▶ **Garoupa** – Grouper (fish such as sea bass)
▶ **Hainan chicken** – Chicken in ginger marinade, served on rice
▶ **Hairy crab** – A delicatessen in autumn and winter, served boiled
▶ **Hot pot** – Meat, fish and vegetable fondue
▶ **Lo hon vegetables** – various vegetables (Buddhist meal during fasting periods)
▶ **Peking duck** – Duck, marinated and roasted in the oven; the crispy skin is the best part
▶ **Wonton** – A noodle-dough dumpling stuffed with shrimp meat, served in broth (photo right)
▶ **Yangchow fried rice** – Fried rice with chicken, egg, peas, shrimp, mushrooms and other ingredients

effected the popularity of this typical tea-house and its unique atmosphere in any way. The ladies pushing the trolleys with dim sums can usually even speak a little English and are happy to help. *2/F City Hall | Edinburgh Place* 愛丁堡廣場 *| tel. 25 2113 03 | Dim sum 11am–3pm, Sun from 9am | Moderate*

ONE HARBOUR ROAD 港灣壹號 ※ **(134 A3)** *(ᗰ E11)*
The most exquisite Cantonese cuisine vies with the panoramic view of the harbour in this restaurant. It is the best place in town for roast duck. The only thing without any inspiration is its name. *Grand Hyatt, 8th floor | tel. 25 84 79 38 | Expensive*

PEKING GARDEN 北京樓
(133 E3) (*C11*)

Peking Duck is this restaurant's speciality but you can also order Beggar's Chicken and dishes from other regions of China. The Noodle Show (at about 8pm every evening) is great fun – spaghetti stretching by hand! *Alexandra House | Chater Rd.* 遮打道 *(MTR exit H) | tel. 25 26 64 56; branch without noodle show: Star House | 3 Salisbury Rd.* 梳士巴利道 *| tel. 27 35 82 11 (130 C6)* (*E9*) *| Moderate*

SHANGHAI GARDEN 紫玉蘭
(133 E3) (*D11*)

Shanghai cuisine classics. 'Drunken Chicken' (in rice-wine sauce) and sautéed shrimps are specialities of the house. *Hutchinson House | 10 Harcourt Rd.* 夏慤道 *| tel. 25 24 81 81 | Moderate*

XI YAN SWEETS 囍宴甜
(134 A4) (*E12*)

The chic restaurant with its large windows in the Star Street district looks more expensive than it is. It serves Chinese-Southeast Asian cooking – and not only deserts as its name might make you believe. You should not miss out on the litchi ice-cream with osmnathus wine. *8 Wing Fung St.* 永豐街 *| tel. 28 33 62 99 | Budget*

YUNG KEE 鏞記 ★
(133 D3) (*C11*)

Absolutely first-class Cantonese cooking. The gigantic restaurant has been owned by the same family since 1942. Also very good for dim sums on Sunday (from 11am). *32–40 Wellington St.* 威靈頓街 *| tel. 25 22 16 24 | Expensive*

YUNYAN 雲陽閣
(130 C4–5) (*E8*)

If you are looking for authentic, spicy Szechuan cooking, this is the right place! Connoisseurs are especially fond of the beef dishes and dumplings – but the duck and mandarin fish are also not to be sneezed at. *4/F Miramar Shopping Centre, 132 Nathan Rd.* 彌敦道 *| tel. 23 75 08 00 | Moderate*

Chopping, frying, steaming: classical Cantonese cooking is celebrated in the restaurant Yung Kee

INTERNATIONAL CUISINE

FARM KITCHEN VEGI 🥗
(131 D5) (∅ F8)

Here, all the food served is very healthy – but not only vegetarian in spite of the name! The spectrum ranges from Italy to Japan. Chic atmosphere. *2/F, The Cameron | 33 Cameron Rd.* 金馬倫道 *| tel. 2721 18 00 | Moderate*

INSIDERTIP ▶ FRINGE GALLERY
藝穗會餐廳 (133 D3) (∅ C12)

Gastronomic added value: a vegetarian lunch buffet is available on the top floor of the Fringe Club at noon. The highlight is the spacious terrace. Make sure to arrive before 2pm if you don't want to have to make do with leftovers. *2 Lower Albert Rd.* 下亞厘畢道 *| Budget*

GAYLORD 爵樂印度餐廳
(130 C5) (∅ E9)

Hong Kong's best known Indian has been delighting his guests since 1972. Vegetarian meals available, elegant atmosphere. *23–25 Ashley Rd.* 亞士厘道 *| tel. 2376 10 01 | Moderate*

INDOCHINE 1929 ★
(133 D3) (∅ C11)

Vietnam's cuisine unites the best of three culinary worlds – French, Southeast Asian and Chinese. You should definitely try the spring rolls wrapped in lettuce leaves, the salt-and-pepper crabs and the wonderful tofu. Inexpensive lunches. *4/F, 21 D'Aguilar Street* 德己立街 *(entrance on Wing Wah Lane* 榮華里*) | tel. 28 69 73 99 | Expensive*

LIFE 🥗
(133 D3) (∅ B11)

The Mediterranean (with a touch of Asian), vegetarian, organic food served here is full of flavour. The fruit juices and inexpensive wine are also good reasons to try out this trendy restaurant in the SoHo district. *10 Shelley St.* 些利街 *| tel. 2810 97 77 | Budget*

INSIDERTIP ▶ NHA TRANG
芽莊越式料理 (133 D2) (∅ C11)

Vietnamese. There is not much room and it always packed; this is the right place to come into contact with people. The atmosphere is dominated by the noise made by the cheerful diners – the food is excellent. No reservations – count on having to wait a while for a table. *88–90 Wellington St.* 威靈頓街 *| Moderate*

LOW BUDGET

▶ *Peoples' kitchen:* Noodle soup, rice soup or Yangzhou fried rice will satisfy you for less than HK$80. A good address is *Tsim Chai Kee | 98 Wellington St., Shop B* (133 D2) (∅ B–C11) – the best of many similar establishments on the same street; it can be recognised by its large windows.

▶ *Lunch:* A good tip in all price categories – you will even be able to afford the gourmet restaurants from Monday to Friday but be there before 1pm; that is when the lunch break begins and it gets very crowded.

▶ 🍴 *City Super:* A cookhouse with a view of the harbour in an air-conditioned shopping emporium – choose your meal, note the number, pay at the cash desk and then order. *Harbour City, Zone A, 3rd floor* (130 B5) (∅ E9)

Dining at The Peak with the magnificent skyline below you

PANASH (130 B–C6) (*⊞ E9*)

Bakery with Italian cooking; the pasta is inexpensive and good. In addition, there are some Japanese dishes, delicious desserts and children's meals. *G 04, Ocean Terminal 海運大廈 | tel. 23 11 04 11 | Budget*

PEAK LOOKOUT 太平山餐廳 ★ (132 C5) (*⊞ B13*)

The most beautiful restaurant in Hong Kong lies hidden in luxuriant greenery opposite Peak Tower. It dazzles its guests with its varied Pan-Asian cooking and – above all – the incomparable atmosphere of an old colonial building with veranda and shady garden. *121 Peak Rd. 山頂道 | tel. 28 49 10 00 | Expensive*

PIZZA EXPRESS (134 A4) (*⊞ D–E12*)

This is not a snack bar but a chic, modern restaurant with a small courtyard. One recommendation is the vegetarian INSIDERTIP Trifolata prepared with truffle oil; it is good enough to make a Neapolitan pizza baker envious. You can choose between three bases: thin, very thin and wholemeal. Several branches. *10 Wing Fung St. 永豐街 (Star Street area) | tel. 35 28 05 41 | www.pizzaexpress.com.hk | Budget–Moderate*

A TOUCH OF SPICE 香辣屋 (130–131 C–D4) (*⊞ E8*)

Thai-Vietnamese cuisine served in a somewhat nostalgic, colonial, friendly environment with wicker chairs. *10 Knutsford Terrace 諾士佛臺 | tel. 23 12 11 18 | www.kingparrot.com | Moderate*

XENRI NO TSUKI 千里之月 (135 D4) (*⊞ G12*)

We have to admit it: this restaurant is nowhere near being inexpensive, but if you want to try the best the Japanese kitchen has to offer, you will pay less here than in other places. Our tip: sit at the bar and watch how the cook creates his works of art. *6/F, Jardine Centre | 50 Jardine's Bazaar 渣甸街 | tel. 25 76 18 80 | Expensive*

SHOPPING

People with only one day in Hong Kong will probably be perfectly happy with a shopping spree in **Stanley**. **Causeway Bay** and **Mong Kok** are the districts where you will find the largest range of items in a small area. Luxury goods are concentrated in **Central**. Avoid the shops in Tsim Sha Tsui near Nathan Road: they are often expensive, dubious tourist traps. **Temple Street night market** is a good address in the cheap to middle-price range.

Of course, Hong Kong is *the* place to shop! But the exorbitant shop rents don't give the dealers much leeway. And not every purchase is a real bargain. Goods from the Far East, especially China, can be recommended. Clothes, bags, accessories and household goods are cheap if you buy them at street markets. Brand names from Europe are only a little cheaper (and sometimes more expensive) than at home and are only sold if they have prestige value in Hong Kong. Alcohol and tobacco are very expensive. There are special discounts on many goods throughout the year and there are no set sales times.

Photo: The Landmark shopping centre

Although this shoppers' paradise has become more expensive, you may well need that extra suitcase when you leave

Only buy high-quality items in specialist shops or from authorised dealers and, best of all, from those with the seal of quality of the Hong Kong Tourism Board (HKTB) – a golden Q with the Chinese symbol for 'Q' inside it: proven quality; knowledge of the article, advice, honesty, etc. You can find a list of these companies, sorted by type of goods sold and district, under *www.discoverhongkong.com/eng/jsp/shopping/search-index.jsp*, from the HKTB visitors' centres or on their hotline: *tel. 25 08 12 34*.

If you intend to buy electrical items (cameras, video or hi-fi equipment, etc.), it is a good idea to know exactly the brand and model you want because the advice given often leaves much to be desired. You can ask the company representatives in Hong Kong for information on recom-

Sai Yeung Choi St. is a good address for electronic goods and cameras

mended sales prices. The HKTB will help you find the right addresses.

Department stores and supermarkets have fixed prices and the same applies to reduced articles. However, discounts are often given in camera and hi-fi shops, if you buy jewellery, watches or similar articles, as well as at street markets; it is simply a matter of your skill at bartering. If you are offered much more than a 10% discount on high-quality goods, you should assume that the dealer is trying to cheat you. There is usually no discount granted if you pay with your credit card. If you do not intend to pay in cash, it is a good idea to say so early on.

Make sure that you are given a globally valid guarantee as well as operating instructions in English if you buy any appliances. Some things are sold cheaper because the guarantee is only valid in Hong Kong; take this into consideration when comparing prices. Do not pay any deposit unless it is only a small amount in one of the shops with the Q sign. However, a first instalment of at least 50 percent is expected for commissioned work (tailors, opticians, etc). Today, Hong Kong is a better place for buying typical Chinese articles

than cut-rate goods. It is more expensive than in China itself, but you will usually get the top export quality. Jade is a classic buy (see 'Jewellery'). Walk No. 1 will show you where to buy household goods from steaming baskets to kitchen cleavers; Walk No. 3 will take you to bric-a-brac and art (see 'Art, antiques & bric-a-brac').

SPECTACLES & CONTACT LENSES

Optical 88 has branches throughout the city. If you want something exceptionally chic, go to *Eye'n-I | 50–52 Queen's Rd. Central* (133 D3) (*∅ C11*). But the real sensation when it comes to price and variety is **INSIDER TIP** *New Fei Optical* on one floor of a factory in Mong Kok: *12/F, Lucky Horse Building | 1–7 Bute St., entrance Arran Lane | www.newfei.com.hk* (128 A6) (*∅ D5*).

BOOKS

SWINDON BOOK CO. (130 C5) (*∅ E9*) Best English bookshop in the city with a wide selection of literature on China and Hong Kong. *13–15 Lock Rd.* 樂道

COMPUTERS

Reasonably priced accessories. The *Star Computer City | Star House, 2nd floor | 3 Salisbury Rd.* (130 C6) (*ꕔ E9*) is centrally located but the INSIDERTIP *Wanchai Computer Centre | 130 Hennessy Rd.* (134 B4) (*ꕔ E12*) and in the *Computer Mall* on the 10th and 11th floors of the *Windsor House | Great George St.* (135 D4) (*ꕔ G12*) has a larger selection and better prices.

SHOPPING CENTRES

Here you can go on a shopping spree in air-conditioned comfort and never get wet. Usually, high-quality goods are sold. The best addresses on the island are the fashionable, but very expensive, *Landmark* (133 D3) (*ꕔ C11*), the hardly any less luxurious, spacious ★ *IFC Mall* (133 D–E2) (*ꕔ C11*) with around 200 shops and restaurants, the 11 sales floors of ★ ● *Times Square* (134 C4) (*ꕔ G12*), with its gigantic atrium and lots of food outlets, as well as the 3-storey *Pacific Place* (133 F3–4) (*ꕔ D12*), with a branch of the Japanese Seibu department store. The most notable centres in Kowloon are the labyrinthine complexes *Ocean Terminal, Ocean Centre* and *Gateway Arcade* that are joined together to form the *Harbour City* (130 B–C 5–6) (*ꕔ D–E9*). It takes hours to just walk past all the shop fronts there. And finally, *Langham Place* (130 C1) (*ꕔ E5*) in Mong Kok is really spectacular.

ELECTRONIC AND OPTICAL EQUIPMENT, CAMERAS

It is hardly worth buying a camera in Hong Kong these days unless you are prepared to do without menu navigation in a language you understand, a two-year guarantee and are willing to accept a charger with the wrong plug. In any case, steer clear of the tourist shops in the Peking Road/Nathan Road area (130 C5) (*ꕔ E9*). It is better to go straight to INSIDERTIP *Sai Yeung Choi Street* south of Nelson Street: there you will find several electronic and camera shops selling current goods at low fixed prices (130 C1) (*ꕔ E5–6*).

The *Fortress* technology market also sells hi-fi and video equipment at reasonable prices. There are branches in all the shopping centres including *Ocean Centre* (130 C5) (*♝ E9*) and on the 7th and 8th floors of *Times Square* (134 C4) (*f G12*). The 3rd floor of the Ocean Centre and 8th floor of Times Square are generally good for home entertainment equipment and cameras. Both have Bose branches. *Standard Audio (Ocean Centre 303–305)* has an excellent sound studio.

Champagne Court is a mini-mall with half a dozen shops for used cameras and lenses including high-quality Leica and Hasselblad equipment. *16 Kimberley Rd.* (130 C5) (*♝ E8*)

Make sure the goods that get packed are those you paid for and don't forget to check that any video equipment is compatible with the standards back home.

DEPARTMENT STORES & SPECIALIST SHOPS

INSIDER TIP ▶ DNA (131 D5) (*♝ F8*)

This is Hong Kong's craziest department store. Three floors of way-out clothing fashions, bags, decorations, shoes, jewellery ... The biggest problem is finding your way out again. *Cameron Rd. 金馬倫道, corner Chatham Rd.*

GOD

Goods of Desire: Here you can buy off-beat furniture and many unusual odds and ends. *30 Canton Rd. 廣東道* (130 C5) (*♝ E9*); *Sharp St. East 霎東街* (134 C4) (*♝ G12*)

INSIDER TIP ▶ HORIZON PLAZA

新海怡廣場 (136 A5) (*♝ B18*)

Warehouse sales on 28 floors! You can buy top fashion inexpensively at *Joyce (21st floor), Armani (22nd floor)* and *Lane Crawford (25th floor);* it is also worth making the long journey for toys and home accessories. You can recover from shopping in the *Tree Café (28th floor). 2 Lee Wing*

St. 利榮街 | *buses 590 from Central, 590A, 90 B from Admiralty to the terminus, then walk or take a taxi*

MUJI 無印良品

This is where simplicity has become a cult. The minimalistic design in this Japanese shop ranges from shirts, to files and champagne glasses to crackers. *3rd floor, Lee Theatre Plaza* | *99 Percival St. 波斯富街* (134 C4) (*♝ G12*); *also Shop 415, Ocean Centre* | *Canton Rd. 廣東道* (130 C5) (*♝ E9*) *and other branches* | *www.muji. com.hk*

PYLONES

If you like playing around with colours, this is the place for you – office equipment, kitchen utensils, lamps, toys and much, much more. *Shop 916A, Times Square 時代廣場* (134 C4) (*♝ G12*); *also Shop 3229, Gateway Arcade* | *Canton Rd. 廣東道* (130 C5) (*♝ E9*)

SHANGHAI TANG 上海灘 ★

(133 D3) (*♝ C11*)

The cheekily colourful Chinese contrast to Muji with classical Chinese women's clothing, as well as material and boxes, cushions and bags, and all kings of odds and ends. *Pedder Building* | *12 Pedder St. 畢打街*

SOGO 崇光百貨

(134–135 C–D4) (*♝ G12*)

Hong Kong's largest Japanese department store: 12 floors of designer fashion, delicatessen, household goods, cosmetics and much more – mostly in the mid-to-high price category. *555 Hennessy Rd. 軒尼詩道*

YUE HWA CHINESE PRODUCTS

裕华国货 (130 C4) (*♝ E7*)

Here you will find almost all the consumer articles China considers fit for export –

from silk cheongsams, massage chairs and Chinese medicines to arts and crafts. International branded articles are also sold. *301–309 Nathan Rd.* 彌敦道

CLOTHING

Leisure and sports clothes are attractively priced. High-quality clothing is usually more expensive than in Europe but you will occasionally come across massively reduced items.

Most of the haute couture boutiques are concentrated in the luxury hotels and shopping centres. The Japanese department stores such as *Sogo* carry a wide range of good-quality clothing in all price categories. ★ *Granville Road* between Carnavon Road and Chatham Road is a magnet for shoppers looking for young fashion, as well as sport and leisure time apparel **(130–131 C–D5)** *(⚏ E–F8)*.

ISLAND BEVERLY 金百利商場, **CAUSEWAY PLACE** 銅鑼灣地帶 **(135 D4)** *(⚏ G12)*

Labyrinth of small boutiques – trendy gear for young people by Hong Kong fashion designers. *Corner East Point Rd.* 東角道*/ Great George St.* 記利佐治街

LADIES' MARKET 女人街 **(130 C1)** *(⚏ E5–6)*

You will not find a great selection of clothes in European sizes (for women and men) at the many stands but there are also accessories and children's wear. Nothing very high-class, but mostly dirt cheap. *Afternoon and evening | Tung Choi St.* 通菜街 *| south of Argyle St.*

LANE CRAWFORD 連卡佛

Elegant department stores with international fashions (also jewellery). *Podium 3 International Finance Centre (IFC)* **(133 E2)**

Street market in Central: this is where bargains can be found

(📖 C11); Pacific Place | 88 Queensway 金鐘道 (133 F3–4) (📖 D12)

INSIDER TIP ▸ PEDDER BUILDING 畢打行 (133 D3) (📖 C11)
Numerous boutiques are hidden away on the upper storeys of one of the last old buildings in Central (Shanghai Tang, see above, is downstairs!) 12 Pedder St. 畢打街

STANLEY MARKET 赤柱市場
(U D6) (📖 0)
Shops and stalls full of ready-made clothes – jeans, silk blouses, pullovers, sportsware and leisure clothes – are clus-

tered together in the centre of the old village in the south of the island. Watch out for fakes! Bus 6 from Exchange Square

SUITCASES & BAGS

Gigantic selection. Good buys in the Chinese department stores and even better ones at the Temple Street Market (130 C3) (📖 E7) and Ladies' Market on Tung Choi Street (130 C1) (📖 E5–6).

ART, ANTIQUES & BRIC-A-BRAC

Beware of imitations! A certificate of authenticity is not necessarily authentic and even serious merchants get taken in sometimes. In spite of all that, you are more likely to get the real thing if you buy in shops with tidy window displays where the individual articles are shown to their advantage.

However, it is also possible to find something you like on the cluttered shelves at the flea market – even if it turns out to be an honest fake. But in that case, it won't have cost a fortune. Modern art from China is very popular at the moment making it well-worth visiting Hong Kong's galleries!

HOLLYWOOD ROAD 荷李活道 AND CAT STREET 摩羅上街 ★
The area where the antique and art dealers do business stretches from the upper end of Wyndham Street (133 E3) (📖 C11) to Possession Street (132 C2) (📖 B11). The spectrum of treasures ranges from porcelain and jade, Buddhist statues, carpets and furniture to ink paintings, lacquer goods and modern art (the latter especially on Wyndham Street). You will have most fun rummaging around on Upper Lascar Row (132 C2) (📖 B11) that is also known as Cat Row. No matter whether Chinese arts

---

LOW BUDGET

▸ Apliu Street flea market: A lot of old odds and ends, but dirt cheap prices for brand-new small articles such as pocket torches, nail clippers, magnifying glasses, toy cars, binoculars ... Daily from noon (128 A4) (📖 C–D 3–4)

▸ Fa Yuen Street: Low prices and the atmosphere of 20 years ago: t-shirts, household goods, toys, underwear, knitwear, children's clothes, stockings, bags, towels, fruit, artificial flowers ... During the day between Prince Edward Rd. and Mong Kok Rd. (128 B5–6) (📖 E5)

▸ The Lanes: Two tiny streets that you would hardly expect to find in Central – stands with clothing, shoes, costume jewellery, bags, material and other bits and pieces at low prices – as long as you know how to barter. During the day | Li Yuen St. East & West (133 D2) (📖 C11)

Stanley and its colourful market are right in the south of Hong Kong Island

and crafts, used household goods or memorabilia from the Mao period, there is always something to discover there. But remember that you will have to bargain. Walk No. 3 takes you to the two streets.

YAN GALLERY 仁畫廊
(133 D3) (🕮 B11)
A peaceful modern-art gallery. *1/F, 1 Hollywood Rd.* 荷李活道

ARTS AND CRAFTS

China's low wages and the country's traditional craftsmanship provide a rich offer of lacquer ware, cloisonné, porcelain, carvings, embroidery, jade jewellery and other exotic goods from the Far East. However, it is frequently rather difficult to recognise the real refinements and elegance of old Chinese art.

CHINESE ARTS AND CRAFTS 中藝 ★
The extensive range of goods makes this gigantic shop Hong Kong's leading place

to purchase non-antique arts and crafts from China. It may be that most articles could be bought for less money elsewhere – especially in China itself – but here, there is the widest of choices and the quality is first rate. *Star House | 3 Salisbury Rd.* 梳士巴利道 **(130 C6) (🕮 E9)**; *China Resources Building | 26 Harbour Rd.* 港灣道 **(134 B4) (🕮 E–F12)**

MARKETS

STANLEY MARKET 赤柱市場 ★
(U D6) (🕮 0)
This market is mainly a source of clothing but there are also many bargains for jewellery, toys, table linen, pictures and pretty arts and crafts. *During the day | buses 6, 6X from Exchange Square*

TEMPLE STREET 廟街 ★
(130 C3) (🕮 E7)
Hong Kong's popular night market is a real attraction. Especially in the southern section, shoppers find an exceptional

range of goods close together: clothing, bags, sunglasses, toys, clocks, new and used electronic appliances. The market continues to the north of Tin Hau Temple. You can eat just like people did years ago in one of the many traditional street cookhouses or daipadongs. Don't forget to walk around the multi-storey car park south of the temple: that is where you will find fortune tellers and amateur musicians giving their all to Cantonese opera. *Daily 6pm to around 11pm.*

FURNITURE & INTERIOR DECORATION

The focus is on the western end of *Queen's Road East (134 A4–5) (⚲ E12)*. You will only find all that the small shops have to offer by looking into their catalogues. Pay special attention to the shops selling redwood cupboards, rattan furniture and furnishing fabrics (gigantic selection of sofa cushions!). You can also purchase Chinese furniture from *Yue Hwa Chinese Products | 301–309 Nathan Rd. (130 C4) (⚲ E7)*.

MUSIC

Be careful about buying cheap CDs at street markets: they are usually miserable pirate pressings.

HMV

You will find just about everything your heart desires in Hong Kong's largest music shop. *Shop UG06, lower level, iSquare | 63 Nathan Rd.* 彌敦道 *(130 C5) (⚲ E9), Central Building | 1–3 Pedder St.* 畢打街 *(133 D3) (⚲ C11) and other branches*

JEWELLERY

Although there is no VAT, jewellery is not always cheaper in Hong Kong than in Europe. Chinese taste has led to its own very special designs. Don't forget that jewellery does not have a great resale value. Gold is less critical: in keeping with Hong Kong law, the purity of gold must be hallmarked (at least 8 carat). The best place to start your search is in one of the renowned jewellers in *Prince's Building (10 Chater Rd./Statue Square) (133 E3) (⚲ C11)*, e.g. in shops 103 *(Supreme)*, 104–105 *(Wai Kee,* with pearls) and *C.Y. Tse* (229) where you will find old Chinese jade jewellery. But if you do want to buy jade, the best place is *Chinese Arts and Crafts (Star House) (130 C6) (⚲ E9)*: the prices are high but the advice is indispensible.

JADE MARKET 玉器市場
(130 C3) (⚲ E7)

More than 400 small dealers offer a kaleidoscope of Chinese jade jewellery in the shadow of the urban motorway. Don't let them palm anything off on you if you are not an expert. *Daily 10am–6pm | corner Kansu St.* 甘肅街*/Reclamation St.* 新填地街

KING FOOK 景福
(133 D2) (⚲ C11)

This long-established chain of specialised shops is particularly recommendable if you want to buy gold jewellery. Excellent advice. *30–32 Des Voeux Rd. Central* 德輔道中 *and other branches*

INSIDER TIP ▶ WING KUT STREET
永吉街 (133 D2) (⚲ B11)

An entire street full of rhinestones and false pearls; but genuine, very beautiful jade jewellery is sold on the upper floor of *house no. 8.*

TAILORS

The goods you get from cheap tailors are usually just a waste of money especially if they have to be made within 24 hours.

Quality has its price in Hong Kong. Place your order at least five days before you plan to leave so that there will be time for two fittings and choose a tailor who works nearby. The tailors in the shopping arcades of the large hotels are accustomed to catering to clients from abroad and have a fine selection of fabrics and fashionable cuts.

An extremely renowned gentlemen's tailor is *W.W. Chan | 2/F, Burlington House, 92 Nathan Rd.* (130 C5) (*ØJ E8–9*). Both men and women will be well catered to at *Mandarin Tailor | 606B, Pedder Building | 12 Pedder St.* (133 D3) (*ØJ C11*).

MATERIAL

You will find a wide range of material, including silk, at *Yue Hwa | 301–309 Nathan Rd.* (130 C4) (*ØJ E7*). Another possibility is at the *Western Market* but you will have to bargain there. *323 Des Voeux Rd. Central* (132 C2) (*ØJ B10–11*)

TEA

The ● INSIDERTIP *Lok Cha Tea Shop* near Cat Street: *288–290 Queen's Rd. Central* (132 C2) (*ØJ B11*); is a particularly charming place to taste and buy teas – perfect for a short break; there is also a branch at the *K. S. Lo Gallery (in the Museum of Tea Ware) | Hong Kong Park* (133 E3) (*ØJ D12*).

The *Fook Ming Tong Tea Shop | 3225, Gateway Arcade, Harbour City* (130 B5) (*ØJ E9*) is another lovely place that caters especially to foreign guests.

CARPETS

CHINESE CARPET CENTRE

This is the place to find a large selection of fine, elegant Chinese carpets. *Houston Centre | 63 Mody Rd.* 麼地道

A kaleidoscope of colours: a stand in the Jade Market

TAI PING CARPETS

Chinese carpets with modern designs. The traditional company's showrooms are small but a visit is always worthwhile. *213 Prince's Building* 太子大廈 *| 10 Chater Rd.* 遮打道/*Statue Square* 皇后像廣場

WATCHES

You will find a gigantic selection of watches ranging from exclusive Swiss brands and fashion watches to imitation Rolexes. You should always buy brand names from an authorised dealer. Another possibility is from one of the many branches of *City Chain* spread throughout Hong Kong. Table or wall clocks can be purchased in the city's department stores.

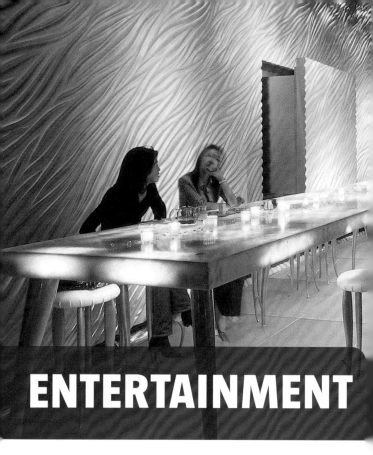

ENTERTAINMENT

CITY WHERE TO START?

The ideal place to be dazzled by the neon glare of the harbour at night is at the south tip of **Kowloon** and the best time is after 8pm to see the laser show. The bar district **Lan Kwai Fong** and the adjacent streets is another must on the Hong Kong side. It's not far from there with the Central Escalator to the restaurants and bars in **SoHo**. The **Temple Street night market** is much more exotic and is easy to reach by underground from the Central Station.

Nightlife in large harbour cities is usually seen as being a bit seedy – this is also true for Hong Kong.

Single male travellers do sometimes get taken in by touts but the truth about Hong Kong at night is that, although things here might be a bit more colourful, they are also extremely civilised and relaxed. Visitors will soon feel at home whether it is at a classic concert or over a glass of beer in an Irish pub. But Chinese cliques – with their love of singing – tend to prefer to keep themselves to themselves when it comes to karaoke.

The public in ★ *Lan Kwai Fong*, the synonym for nightlife in Hong Kong,

Bars, jazz and open-air opera: no matter whether it is Chinese music or a nightclub, you'll be certain to find something you like

comes from all walks of life. The upper end of D'Aguilar Street is closed to traffic at night and this is where tourists find a lively mixture of bars, pubs and the more elegant restaurants (133 D3) (*ω C11–12*).

The second hotspot is *Soho* 'South of Hollywood Road'. There are many restaurants – some of them are also bars – here on both sides of the Central Escala-

tor near Staunton Street and Shelley Street (133 D3) (*ω B11*). An alternative off-scene has developed on the western fringe along INSIDER TIP *Peel Street*.

The third hub is the most famous: the Wan Chai area (134 A4) (*ω E12*) that is not even half as disreputable as its reputation would have you believe.

Car-free INSIDER TIP *Knutsford Terrace* in Tsim Sha Tsui is a small-scale version of

High above the hustle and bustle between skyscrapers: chilling out in a rooftop garden

Lan Kwai Fong (130–131 C–D4) (𝄞 E8). The panorama of the harbour at night seen from the south of Kowloon near the Cultural Centre (130 C6) (𝄞 E9) never fails to impress. The absolute highlight is the ★ *Symphony of Lights* that takes place every evening at around 8pm. Laser projectors on 67 skyscrapers on both sides of the harbour transform it into a theatre of light accompanied by music on the promenade and opposite the Convention & Exhibition Centre, and it is made even more exciting on certains days by fireworks displays.

Or, you can join the Hong Kongers: their idea of after-work fun is to flock to department stores and boutiques, cinemas and restaurants, in INSIDER TIP Causeway Bay or to meet for a tête-à-tête in neighbouring Victoria Park. Go for a stroll and take in the atmosphere of Hong Kong; nowhere else is it more typical. (134–135 C–D 3–4) (𝄞 F–G 11–12)

If you feel that the evening might get to be a bit boozy, it is a good idea to take your credit cards out of your wallet and pay cash for your drinks as you order them. But careful: alcohol is very expensive!

AQUA SPIRIT ★ ☼
(130 C5–6) (𝄞 E9)

The bar to end all bars, with all of Hong Kong at your feet. What a panorama! Something else will also make you stare in wonder – the prices in the right column of the list of beverages. Everything here is unforgettable. *30th floor | 1 Peking Rd.* 北京道

INSIDER TIP ► CLUB 71
(133 D2) (𝄞 B11)

The New York Times described this inexpensive pub as 'the antithesis of a Philippe Starck watering hole' meaning that here design is not as important as discussion. This is where journalists, film people and bohemians get together in a laid-back atmosphere. There are also a few tables outside. *67 Hollywood Rd.* 荷李活道 *(at the back, entrance via Peel Street)*

LA DOLCE VITA (133 D3) (𝄞 C12)

Nomen est omen: the bar – with curves that Anita Ekberg would be proud of – forces its way out onto the street. A place to see and be seen. *9 Lan Kwai Fong* 蘭桂坊

FELIX ★ (130 C6) *(E9)*
A completely different galaxy. This way-out creation designed by Philippe Starck calls itself a restaurant but the glass-floored bars and the breathtaking views at twilight are much more fantastic than the expensive food. Green mini-discotheque *Crazy Box*. Another highlight: the WCs. *Entrance from the western shopping arcade | The Peninsula | Salisbury Road 梳士巴利道*

FRINGE CLUB ROOFTOP GARDEN
藝穗會餐廳 (133 D3) *(C12)*
Do you feel like you need a break although you're not really tired? Then the rooftop garden of the Fringe Club is the place to go. In the evening the photo gallery serves tapas and drinks. *2 Lower Albert Road 下亞厘畢道*

MES AMIS
The Chinese and western clientele are especially fond of the spacious Wan Chai branch with its long, open front and an impressive collection of bottles over the bar. You can also eat here. DJs on Wed, Fri and Sat; free sparkling wine 'for the fairer sex' is served after 10pm on Wed – Ladies' Night! Happy hour with reduced prices for drinks runs until 9pm every day and even one hour longer at the weekend. *83 Lockhart Rd., corner Luard Rd. 駱克道/盧押道 (134 A4) (E12); also 15 Ashley Rd. 亞士厘道 (130 C5) (E9)*

INSIDER TIP **PEEL FRESCO MUSIC LOUNGE** (133 D2–3) *(B11)*
Real aficionados play jazz, funk, etc. here beneath baroque paintings in gold frames. Reasonable prices. *49 Peel St. 卑利街*

POST 97 (133 D3) *(C12)*
Whether serious or flipped out: Even 'post 1997' everybody feels good in the most popular pub/restaurant in Lan Kwai Fong. This is where everything is just right: the inviting interior, the international cooking, the mixture of guests. *No. 9–11 蘭桂坊*

SKYLARK (133 D3) *(C11)*
The Skylark's house band plays jazz and R&B; sometimes an admission fee is

MARCO POLO HIGHLIGHTS

★ **Lan Kwai Fong**
A magnet in the evening: bar and restaurant district with a special flair → p. 74

★ **Symphony of Lights**
The curtain goes up on the world's largest *son et lumière* show! → p. 76

★ **Aqua Spirit**
Expensive drinks and a panorama worth its weight in gold → p. 76

★ **Felix**
Galactic: Philippe Starck's cabinet → p. 77

★ **Temple Street**
Music at the night market → p. 79

Dance show in Club Bboss: an evening in this club can be very expensive

charged when guest groups perform. The prices are absolutely reasonable. A tip: try the delicious Skylark Martini. *1F, 63 Wyndham St.* 雲咸街

WEINSTUBE (130 C5) (*ɲ E9*)

That's its name but you will probably hear more Cantonese and English in this cheerful little restaurant than German and more beer than wine is quaffed. However, the food served is very German! *22 Ashley Rd.* 亞士厘道

NIGHTCLUBS & DISCOTHEQUES

Be warned: if you are not fashionably dressed you won't make it through the door!

CLUB BBOSS 大富豪夜總會 (131 D5) (*ɲ F8*)

The largest and most famous of Hong Kong's hostess clubs. The luxury creatures in this nightclub owe their existence to China's courtesan tradition and expense-account big spenders. Its special features: extravagant interior decoration with dance floors, bands and floorshows, bars and karaoke, as well as hostesses you can talk to, buy a drink and dance with. But be careful: every 15 minutes will make a dent in your finances! The Club Bboss (pronounced: Biboss) employs more than 1000 first-class hostesses on its 70,000ft² premises: an electric convertible chauffeurs guests along a glittering street – the club is out of this world and so are the prices. *Daily from 1pm | New Mandarin Plaza | 14 Science Museum Rd.* 科學館道

HOME (133 D3) (*ɲ B11*)

Things only really get going here in the early hours of the morning – the final stop for those who can really take a lot after the other discos have closed their doors. *Tue–Sat | basement, 17–19 Hollywood Rd.* 荷李活道 *| www.home-base.hk*

MAKUMBA (133 D2–3) (*ɲ B11*)

This dance hall calls itself an 'African bar lounge' and things really heat up when genuine Afro-Caribbean live music is played: reggae, Afro jazz, etc. Loud! *Tue–Sat | 48 Peel St.* 卑利街

VOLAR (133 D3) (*ɲ C11*)

Dance club with top DJs who play hip-hop, house and soul. 'Time Out' called this the best club in town. The only problem is getting in! *Mon–Sat | 38–44 D'Aguilar St. 德己立街 | www.volar.com.hk*

THEATRE, CONCERTS & BALLET

Today, Hong Kong presents a wide range of noteworthy international cultural events at a variety of venues. However, it is often very difficult for local performers to assert themselves in the face of international guest stars. The cultural boom began in 1975 with the founding of the Philharmonic Orchestra; this was followed four years later by the Hong Kong Ballet. Now, there is also a Chinese orchestra, a theatre ensemble and many small, amateur groups.

ARTS CENTRE 藝術中心
(134 A4) (🗺 E12)

The complex organises a highly varied assortment of theatre, cinema, exhibitions and concerts and plays a major role in Hong Kong's cultural life. *2 Harbour Rd. 港灣道 | tel. 25 82 02 00*

CITY HALL 大會堂 *(133 E3) (🗺 D11)*
The City Hall acts as a venue for cultural and other events. There are concerts and theatre performances almost every day. *Edinburgh Place 愛丁堡廣場 | tel. 29 21 28 40*

CULTURAL CENTRE 文化中心
(130 C6) (🗺 E9)

Hong Kong's most modern and important venue has a concert hall (with Asia's largest pipe organ), a theatre and a studio theatre. *10 Salisbury Rd. 梳士巴利道 | tel. 27 34 20 09 and 27 34 28 49*

INSIDER TIP FRINGE CLUB 藝穗會
(133 D3) (🗺 C12)

This active cultural organisation provides a forum for contemporary, experimental creativity with theatre, performances, music, exhibitions and much, much more.

2 Lower Albert Rd. 下亞厘畢道 | tel. 25 21 72 51 | www.hkfringeclub.com

SUNBEAM THEATRE 新光劇院
(135 F2) (🗺 0)

Hong Kong's only permanent theatre for Cantonese – and other Chinese – opera. Note: performances are not modified in any way for Westerners and many find the music hard to digest! *Performances usually at 7.30pm | 423 King's Rd. 英皇道 | tel. 25 63 29 59*

TEMPLE STREET 廟街 ★ ●
(130 C3) (🗺 E7)

Every evening there is open-air musical fun around the edge of this bustling market. Amateur and semi-professional musicians give all they've got in scenes from Cantonese operas and other Chinese folk music on the south side of Tin Hau Temple – without scenery and free of charge (donations welcome!) Next to them, there is a row of fortune tellers – mainly physiognomists and palmists. Some others work with trained birds. *Daily from around 7pm | Market Street 街市街 (at the multi-storey car park)*

LOW BUDGET

▶ Take advantage of the happy hour! The days when most bars sold two drinks for the price of one are over but there is at least a discount. Many bars start their happy hour when they open their doors. This can last until 9am – much longer than just one hour!

▶ *Ladies' Night*: most discos in Hong Kong offer 'the fairer sex' free admission and free sparkling wine on one night in the week (often Wed).

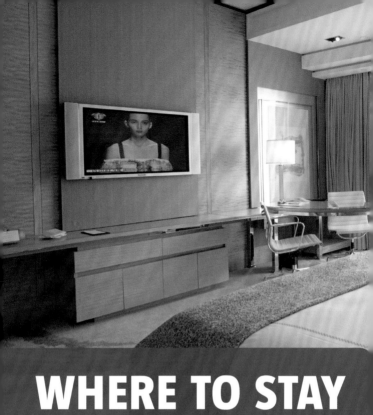

WHERE TO STAY

Hong Kong's hotel industry has high standards. Even in simple guesthouses, air conditioning, a private bathroom, telephone and colour television are a matter of course, as well as a restaurant or coffeeshop serving international dishes from early in the morning until late at night.

Even middle-of-the-range hotels often have a business centre and 24-hour service. In exclusive hotels there are more than two employees per room. However, real luxury in Hong Kong is not as much a matter of service or decoration as one of the liberal use of the rarest and most expensive commodity here: space. Rooms in hotels that

are not top category are correspondingly much less spacious. Sometimes it can even be a problem to find a space for a large suitcase in a room.

As a rule, the comfort offered corresponds with the size of the hotel. 'Good things come in small packages' is almost unknown in Hong Kong. Of course, rooms with a view of the harbour are particularly popular but they are mostly found in luxury hotels. The 'Executive', 'Club' or similarly named floors with extra service, such as breakfast in your room, free tea and coffee, and broadband internet access, are aimed more at business people. Hong Kong hotels are expensive – just how

Pleasant dreams: from luxury suites to hostels in leafy surroundings – the spectrum is wide and the standard often exceptionally high

expensive depends on the date. The top hotels in particular have room rates that sometimes change daily depending on demand; in middle-of-the-range hotels prices change with the season.

This guidebook classifies hotels based on the rates offered by internet booking services and includes the extra 10% 'service charge' levied in Hong Kong. If you book directly at a hotel, you often have to pay more; if you compare prices and are flexible time-wise you can frequently profit from considerable reductions in superior hotels. Inexpensive guesthouses on the other hand often have no leeway for offering lower rates.

You can find out more about most hotels under *www.discoverhongkong.com/eng/ trip-planner/accommodations.html*. All licensed hotel and guesthouse owners

The Intercontinental spoils its guests with a view of the harbour and excellent food

are listed under *www.hadla.gov.hk/en/ hotels*.

HOTELS: EXPENSIVE

Air conditioning, private bathrooms, telephone and broadband internet access in the rooms and suites; WiFi, several restaurants (usually with Chinese and international food), coffeeshop and bar, business centre, conference rooms, hotel doctor, laundry service, babysitters, hotel video programme and travel agency are all standard in hotels in this category. Most also have a hairdresser's and gym.

EXCELSIOR 怡東酒店 ⚘
(135 D3) (⑰ G11)
Gigantic building in the lively Causeway Bay district, unobstructed view of the harbour, nightclub, tennis court. 887 rooms (also for non-smokers). *281 Gloucester Rd. 告士打道 | tel. 28 94 88 88 | www.excelsiorhongkong.com*

GRAND STANFORD
海景嘉福酒店 ⚘ *(131 D5) (⑰ F9)*
More than half of the 578 rooms in this hotel have a harbour view. The gym and swimming pool on the roof provide everything needed for your daily workout. *70 Mody Rd. 麼地道 | tel. 27 21 51 61 | www.hongkong.intercontinental.com*

HYATT REGENCY 尖沙咀凱悅酒店
(130–131 C–D5) (⑰ E9)
This hotel with 381 rooms occupies the 3rd to 24th floors of the K11 skyscraper; beneath is a shopping centre with direct access to the underground. Business people value the INSIDER TIP Club Floors with free WiFi, a private lounge and additional working space. *18 Hanoi Rd. 河内道 | tel. 23 11 12 34 | www.hyatt.com*

INTERCONTINENTAL ★ ⚘
(130–131 C–D6) (⑰ E9)
This hotel not only attracts guests due to its fantastic location on the southern tip

of Kowloon – there is even a view of the harbour from some bathrooms – but also thanks to its excellent gastronomy. The hotel has 495 rooms including 87 suites. *18 Salisbury Rd. 梳士巴利道 | tel. 2721 1211 | www.intercontinental.com*

LANGHAM 朗廷酒店 (130 C5) (*◫ E9*)
Central location in Tsim Sha Tsui, virtually no views of the harbour but 500 pleasant rooms with spacious bathrooms and an excellent Health Club. *8 Peking Rd. 北京道 | tel. 2375 1133 | www.langhamhotels.com*

MARCO POLO HONG KONG HOTEL
馬哥孛羅香港酒店 ☼
(130 C6) (*◫ E9*)
This is a time-honoured hotel in a prime location at the tip of Kowloon next to the Star Ferry. Unobstructed view of the harbour from most of the 667 rooms. *3 Canton Rd. 廣東道 | tel. 2113 0088 | www.marcopolohotels.com*

HOTELS: MODERATE

Standard facilities in this category include: air-conditioning and suites with private bathrooms as well as direct-dial telephones, a restaurant and coffeeshop, bar, business centre, laundry service and excursion booking desk.

CENTRAL PARK HOTEL 中環麗柏酒店
(132 C2) (*◫ B11*)
Light pastel colours dominate the 142 rooms of this chic hotel pleasantly located between Hollywood Park and the antique shop area. *263 Hollywood Rd. 荷李活道 | tel. 2850 8899 | www.centralparkhotel.com.hk*

THE CITYVIEW 城景國際
(130 C2) (*◫ E6*)
Nomen est omen: views of the jungle of skyscrapers can be had from the 413 rooms. The former YMCA has now been refurbished to 4-star luxury standards and has a swimming pool, a large gym and even a prayer room. *23 Waterloo Road 窩打老道 | tel. 2783 3888 | www.thecityview.com.hk*

EMPIRE HOTEL 灣仔皇悅酒店
(134 A4) (*◫ E12*)
276 rooms on 12 floors in the centre of the lively Wan Chai district only a short walk from the Arts Centre and Congress Centre. There is a small roof-top pool. *33 Hennessy Rd. 軒尼詩道 | tel. 3692 2111 | www.empirehotel.com.hk*

GARDEN VIEW YWCA 女青園景軒 ★
(133 D4) (*◫ C12*)
Guests have a view over the zoo to the skyscrapers in the Central District from many of the 141 rooms (including 25 family suites) in this modest-sized tower with

---

★ **Intercontinental**
Front row, panoramic view of the harbour – in South Kowloon
→ p. 82

★ **Garden View YWCA**
A good choice for price-conscious guests; can be reached by the Peak tram → p. 83

★ **Royal Pacific Hotel and Towers**
Comfortable hotel between Kowloon Park and the harbour
→ p. 85

★ **The Salisbury YMCA of Hong Kong**
Family hotel in a prime location with many leisure activities
→ p. 85

MARCO POLO HIGHLIGHTS

a swimming pool, gym, business centre and restaurant. You can walk downhill through the zoo (there is direct access) and take the Peak Tram back up. The hotel belongs to the YWCA but is open to all. Price: at the lower end of this category. *1 Macdonnell Rd.* 麥當勞道 *| tel. 2877 3737 | hotel.ywca.org.hk*

HOLIDAY INN EXPRESS
銅鑼灣智選假日酒店
(134 C4) (*ଞ G12*)
Inexpensive accommodation in Causeway Bay on a peaceful side street! The 282 rooms are relatively spacious – by Hong Kong standards. *33 Sharp St. East* 霎东街 *| tel. 35586688 | www.hiexpress.com*

LUXURY HOTELS

The standard price for the cheapest rooms is at least HK$3700 per night

Four Seasons 四季酒店
(133 D2) (*ଞ C11*)
Hong Kong's premiere luxury hotel with the atmosphere and facilities of a health resort: 22,000ft² spa oasis! The 399 rooms have plasma televisions and DVD players. Direct access to the airport train. You only have to leave the building if you want to play golf. *8 Finance St.* 金融街 *| tel. 31968888 | www.fourseasons.com/ hongkong*

Island Shangri La
港島香格裡拉大酒店
(133 F4) (*ଞ D12*)
This hotel breaks all records: the atrium is 17 storeys high and is decorated with the world's largest Chinese painting (14 storeys). The 566 rooms have higher ceilings than usual to allow enough space for the chandeliers! *Supreme Court Rd.* 法院道 *| tel. 28773838 | www.shangri-la. com/island*

Mandarin Oriental 文華東方酒店
(133 E3) (*ଞ C11*)
A luxury liner on dry land! The spa area combines Chinese medicine, Ayurveda and Kneipp treatments. 502 rooms and

suites up to 3150ft² in size. ● Drinking tea in the hall is a wonderful way to pass the time of day; Hong Kong ladies like to recover here after a day's shopping. *5 Connaught Rd. Central* 干諸道中 *| tel. 25220111 | www.mandarinoriental.com/ hongkong*

The Peninsula 半島酒店
(130 C6) (*ଞ E9*)
A Hong Kong superstar; absolute luxury – especially in the skyscraper wing. Hi-fi equipment in the rooms, bathrooms with television and panoramic views. The hotel's Rolls Royce fleet is almost legendary. 300 rooms including the most expensive suite in Hong Kong – HK$68,000 a night. *Salisbury Rd.* 梳士巴利道 *| tel. 29202888 | www. peninsula.com*

Ritz-Carlton
麗思卡爾頓酒店 ⚜
(130 A4) (*ଞ C8*)
Located on the 102nd–118th floors of the International Commerce Center, this noble 302-roomed hotel is currently the tallest on earth. Of course, there is a wonderful view from all the windows – even when you go swimming on the 116th floor. *1 Austin Rd.* 柯士甸道西 *| tel. 22632263 | www.ritzcarlton.com*

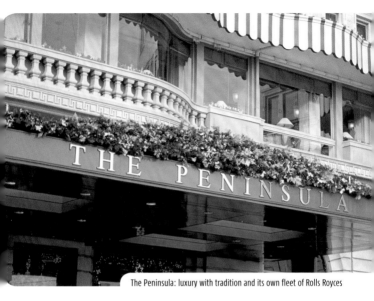

The Peninsula: luxury with tradition and its own fleet of Rolls Royces

HOLIDAY INN GOLDEN MILE
金域假日酒店 (130 C5) (*E9*)
Well-established hotel with 600 rooms in the heart of Tsim Sha Tsui. The *Delicatessen Corner* in the basement serves German-Austrian food. *50 Nathan Rd. 彌敦道 | tel. 23 69 31 11 | www.goldenmile.com*

KOWLOON HOTEL 九龍酒店
(130 C5–6) (*E9*)
Cheaper subsidiary of the Peninsula Hotel in a fine location behind the latter. 736 rooms (also for non-smokers) that are small but equipped with useful information terminals and broadband Wi-Fi. *19–21 Nathan Rd. 彌敦道 | tel. 29 29 28 88 | www.harbour-plaza.com/klnh*

INSIDER TIP ▶ L'HOTEL
銅鑼灣海景酒店 (135 E3) (*H11*)
275 modern rooms in a 40-storey tower near the underground and Victoria Park. The main attraction is the swimming pool on the roof – with a panoramic view of the harbour. *18 King's Rd. 英皇道 | tel. 35 53 28 98 | www.lhotelcausewaybayhv.com*

ROYAL PACIFIC HOTEL AND TOWERS
皇家太平洋酒店 ★
(130 B–C5) (*D–E8*)
675 rooms – some with a view of the sea – in a prime location between the harbour and Kowloon Park (with direct access). You can go to the shopping centre without putting a foot outside. Gym, squash. *China Hong Kong City | 33 Canton Rd. 廣東道 | tel. 27 36 11 88 | www.royalpacific.com.hk*

THE SALISBURY YMCA OF HONG KONG 基督教青年會 ★ ☀
(130 C6) (*E9*)
Intelligently planned, comfortable hotel. 365 rooms, kindergarten, swimming pool area, gym, comprehensive programme of sports and courses, non-smoker floors – and all in a luxurious location next to the Peninsula (many rooms with a harbour view). The perfect choice for families with

children. *41 Salisbury Rd.* 梳士巴利道 | *tel. 22 68 70 00* | *www.ymcahk.org.hk*

STANFORD HILLVIEW HOTEL
仕德福山景酒店 (131 D4) (*ⅢⅢ E8*)

177 rooms in a surprisingly tranquil, green section of the tourist district. *13–17 Observatory Rd.* 天文臺道 | *tel. 27 22 78 22* | *www.stanfordhillview.com*

HOTELS: BUDGET

Standard facilities in this category include: air-conditioning and suites with private bathroom and telephone, as well as a coffeeshop or simple restaurant, laundry service and usually an excursion booking desk.

HOTEL BENITO 華國酒店
(130 C5) (*ⅢⅢ E9*)

New and modern hotel with 74 small rooms in a central location. Free internet (plug-in) but no restaurant. *7–7B Cameron Rd.* 金馬倫道 | *tel. 36 53 03 88* | *www. hotelbenito.com*

BOOTH LODGE 卜維廉賓館
(130 C2) (*ⅢⅢ E7*)

54 rooms in a cheerful little hotel run by the Salvation Army. Centrally located, but peaceful. A pleasant surprise: the charming **INSIDER TIP** restaurant with a balcony and view into the greenery. *11 Wing Sing Lane* 永星里 | *tel. 27 71 92 66* | *boothlodge. salvation.org.hk*

CARITAS BIANCHI LODGE
明愛白英奇賓館 (130 C2–3) (*ⅢⅢ E7*)

Booth Lodge's neighbour: a hotel with 90 rooms in a quiet side street off Nathan Road. *4 Cliff Rd.* 石壁道 | *tel. 23 88 11 11* | *www.caritas-chs.org.hk*

CARITAS LODGE 明愛賓館
(128–129 C–D5) (*ⅢⅢ F4*)

Similar to Bianchi Lodge, but less expensive and more conveniently located. 40 rooms, discount for stays of over one week. *134 Boundary St.* 界限街 | *tel. 23 39 37 77* | *www.caritas-chs.org.hk*

INSIDER TIP CITADINES 馨樂庭亞士厘
服務公寓 (130 C5) (*ⅢⅢ E9*)

Apartment hotel for self caterers. The 36 studios (390–625ft²) are equipped with a kitchen. The prices are at the upper limit for this category. *18 Ashley Rd.* 亞士厘道 | *reservation tel. 22 62 30 62* | *www.cita dines.com*

LOW BUDGET

▶ The most important tip for anyone who plans to stay longer than two or three days: ask for a reduced weekly rate!

▶ *New Lucky House:* There is a selection of pleasant guesthouses on the individual floors of the building on the corner of Nathan Road; the rooms have private bathrooms and some are air conditioned: from HK$300, e.g. *Ocean Guest House (11/F | tel. 23 85 01 25)* or *Hakkas Guest House (3/F | tel. 27 71 36 56). 5 Jordan Rd.* **(130 C4) (*ⅢⅢ E7*)**

▶ *Star Guest House* and *Lee Garden Guest House:* These two are just a little bit better than the others in Tsim Sha Tsui. The 55 rooms have windows, telephone, TV and free air conditioning. Double rooms from HK$500. *21 and 36 Cameron Rd.* | *tel. 27 23 89 51 and 23 67 22 84 respectively* | *www.starguesthouse. com.hk* **(131 D5) (*ⅢⅢ E9*)**

DORSETT SEAVIEW 帝豪海景酒店
(130 C3) (*∅ E7*)

Only a few of the 268 rooms actually have a – distant – sea view but guests here have a comfortable stay in a district full of local colour next to Tin Hau Temple in Yau Ma Tei. *268 Shanghai St. 上海街 | tel. 27 82 08 82 | www.dorsettseaview.com.hk*

THE HARBOUR VIEW 灣景國際 ≈
(134 A4) (*∅ E12*)

Interesting location between the Arts Centre and Convention Centre. 144 of the 320 rooms have an inexpensive view of the harbour. At the top of the category and sometimes even a bit above but discounts are given for longer stays. *4 Harbour Rd. 港灣道 | tel. 28 02 01 11 | www.theharbour view.com.hk*

IBIS NORTH POINT 宜必思世紀軒
(135 F1) (*∅ 0*)

Skyscraper with ferry and tram access, 275 small but modern rooms. *138 Java Rd. 渣華道 | tel. 25 88 11 11 | www.accor hotels.com*

LARGOS HOTEL 朗逸酒店
(130 C3) (*∅ E7*)

Cheerful hotel in a central, fairly quiet, location. Most of the 100 rooms are small but have internet. *30 Nanking St. 南京街 | tel. 27 83 82 33 | www.largos.com.hk*

WHERE TO STAY OUTSIDE THE CITY CENTRE

INSIDER TIP ▶ CONCERTO INN
浪濤軒 (U A6) (*∅ 0*)

Feel like a beach holiday? This well-kept guesthouse with 8 rooms with balconies on Lamma Island 1.5km (1mi) from the village of Yung She Wan (ferry stop) is right on the beach. Peaceful and inexpensive during the week; cannot be recommended on Sat. *28 Hung Shing Ye Beach 洪聖爺灣 |*

A day at the beach at Warwick Hotel

tel. 29 82 16 68 | www.concertoinn.com.hk | Budget

YOUTH HOSTELS

Hong Kong's 7 youth hostels are all located in rural surroundings – the location and furnishings of 6 of them make them only suitable for hikers and people on outings. The lovely complex on Mount Davis (U A3) (*∅ 0*) is completely different (with doubles and family rooms). The hostel has a shuttle bus 4 times a day from and to Shun Tak Centre. *Overnight stay with Youth Hostel ID from HK$100 (double room HK$300) | tel. 28 17 57 15 | www.yha.org.hk | www.hihostels.com*

WARWICK HOTEL 華威酒店
(138 C5) (*∅ 0*)

This comfortable hotel with a bar, restaurants and swimming pool is located right on the beach. The 66 rooms all have balconies. It is only a 10-min. walk to the harbour. Reduced rates during the week. *East Bay, Cheung Chau 長洲東灣 | tel. 29 81 00 81 | www.warwickhotel.com.hk | Moderate*

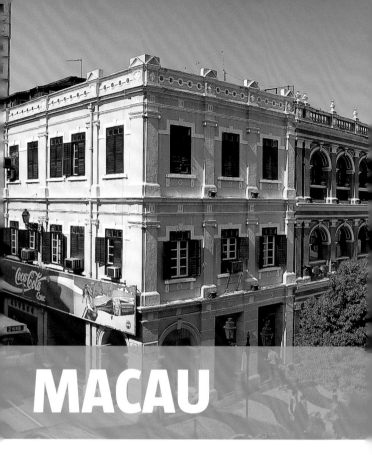

MACAU

CITY WHERE TO START?
Largo do Senado (144 C4)
(⑭ c4): Before you get hooked on gambling, take a look at the historical centre – most attractions in the Old Town can easily be reached on foot from Senate Square. The buses on Largo do Senado can take you to more distant locations and the islands.

MAP INSIDE BACK COVER
From Hong Kong to Portugal in an hour? Hydrofoils really don't take longer than that to cover the 65km (40mi) across the estuary of the Pearl River.

The former Portuguese overseas province was founded in 1557 as a trade and mission station and is the oldest European settlement in East Asia. 550,000 people live here on one third of the area of Hong Kong Island. Macau existed in a kind of limbo for decades until the airport was opened in 1995 and, shortly after that, the casino licenses were handed over to new operators. What visitors see today is a curious mixture of a medium-sized Chinese town, a small Portuguese settlement and a bombastic Las Vegas although Macau has now outstripped the

Photo: Largo do Senado

Churches and casinos: Europe's oldest outpost in the Far East cultivates its traditions and its reputation as the gambling capital

original in the USA in terms of turnover from gambling.

As early as in 1976, Portugal changed Macau's status and declared it Chinese territory under its administration. The city was returned officially to China on 20 December, 1999. Although Portuguese is still the official language along with Chinese, English is much more important as a second language.

Those who prefer to hang on to their money rather than support the gambling industry will be more attracted by the highlights from the European colonial past. Almost all important historical buildings have been restored including some from a period long before Hong Kong even existed.

25 historical buildings have been declared ★ *Unesco World Heritage Sites (www.*

The venerable racing cars in the Grand Prix Museum will make motorsport fans' hearts beat faster

wh.mo) as witnesses to the early interaction between the East and West. They include the São Paulo Ruins, Protestant Cemetery, Guia Fort, A Ma Temple (Ma Kok Miu), the buildings around Largo do Senado, as well as several other churches and temples. Detailed information (with an interactive layout plan) can be found under *www.macauheritage.net*.

SIGHTSEEING

It is best to explore the historical centre around Town Hall Square, *Largo do Senado*, as far as the Protestant Cemetery on foot. It is also worth walking around the southern tip (with the Museu Maritimo and A Ma Temple). The Guia Hill and Jardim de Lou Lim Ieoc are also within walking distance of each other. You can find well thought-out suggestions for INSIDER TIP strolls under *portal.gov.mo/web/guest/tourist* (menu: 'Sightseeing/Walking Tours') – complete with maps and descriptions in English.

COLOANE 路環 ★
(146–147 B–E 4–6) (*Ø b–e 10–12*)
The government decreed that this rural island should remain casino-free. It also has Macau's only bathing beaches. *Cheoc Van Beach* in the south lies in a park and has a swimming pool and restaurant/bar. *Hac Sa Beach* in the east has dark sand and a swimming pool; it is located next to the golf course. The island's newest visitor attraction can be found in *Seac Pai Van Park* on the road from the north of the island to Coloane village: an enclosure for two giant pandas that the Chinese government presented to Macau to commemorate the first 10 years of its 'homecoming' *(www.macaupanda.org.mo)*. The tip of the island is dominated by a monumental statue of Tin Hau or A Ma, the patron saint of mariners, together with the obligatory opulently decorated temple. The INSIDER TIP *village of Coloane* has kept its traditional appearance. It is only a few yards from the bus stop to the water – on the way, you will pass Lord Stow's bakery that sells delicious cream cakes, *pasteis*

de natas. Take the street on the left to *St Francisco Xavier Church.* The monument in front of the building commemorates the victory the villagers had over pirates who had abducted their children in 1910. *Café Nga Tim* on the corner near the church serves typical Macanese dishes. Follow the road along the coast until you reach *Tam Kung Temple* at the end. On the way back, take the small street that runs parallel to the shore from the church near Café Nga Tim where you will find some interesting shops. Then go back to the shore road which leads northwards to as series of shipyards where traditional wooden junks used to be made. Today, however, very few are built. *Buses 15, 21A, 25, 26A.*

COTAI 路氹城
(146–147 B-D 2–4) (*[]* b-d 8–10)

The Las Vegas of the East is being developed on the newly reclaimed land between the islands of Coloane and Taipa. You will be astonished at the two complexes that already exist; others are under construction and will possibly already be open for business when you arrive.

The bombastic ★ ● *Venetian (www.venetianmacao.com)* will immediately catch your eye. When it was opened in 2007, it dwarfed the rest of Macau – 2900 hotel suites, 350 shops, more than 25 acres for conferences and exhibitions, a theatre for shows, a 15,000 seat arena, the world's largest casino with 850 gambling tables and much more – not to forget, the Campanile, Rialto Bridge, Doge's Palace and the possibility to ride in a genuine gondola through an air-conditioned fake Venice! And, the neo-baroque kitsch in the interior is even more 'spectacular' than the outside.

The entrance to the ● *City of Dreams* is opposite the Doge's Palace. In addition to the obligatory casino and shopping arcade, there are three hotels, a 2000-seat theatre (with 'The House of Dancing Water' show every evening) and the *Bubble*, a dome-shaped theatre where a 20-minute visual extravaganza 'Dragon's Treasure' is shown (noon–6pm every half hour; 6pm–10pm hourly). *Free buses to the City of Dreams from Hotel Sintra* (144 C4) (*[]* c4) *(to the west of the Grand Lisboa Hotel) every 15–30 mins. from around 8.30am–10pm; or city buses 15, 21A, 25, 26A*

FISHERMAN'S WHARF
漁人碼頭 (145 E4–5) (*[]* e4–5)

'Real beauty is always somewhere else' and that is what you will feel here when you walk from the ruins of a Roman amphitheatre through rows of houses imitating Amsterdam, New Orleans, Cape Town and Lisbon – all 'originals' from 2005 with shops, restaurants, amusement arcades, a casino and hotel.

★ **Unesco World heritage Sites**
The historic face of the city
→ p. 89

★ **Coloane**
Rural island with Macau's only beach for swimming → p. 90

★ **The Venetian**
Air-conditioned Canal Grande: the casino of superlatives → p. 91

★ **Macau Museum and Fortaleza do Monte**
The charming presentation in this museum in a mighty fortress is the best introduction to old Macau → p. 94

★ **The House of Dancing Water**
The spectacular show in the City of Dreams → p. 98

MARCO POLO HIGHLIGHTS

GRAND PRIX MUSEUM 大賽車博物館 ● AND WINE MUSEUM 葡萄酒博物館 (145 D4) (*ω d4*)

Original racing cars, photos, videos and other documents tell the story of the car and motorbike races that have been held since 1954. The highlight is a 'ride' in the INSIDER TIP▸ driving simulator. Next door, photos and equipment inform visitors of the Portuguese winegrowers' art.

GUIA HILL 松山 ☼
(145 D3–4) (*ω d3–4*)

In 1638, a fortress was built on the highest point in Macau. Since 1865, it has been towered over by a lighthouse, the *Farol da Guia*. There is a pretty little chapel next to it.

HISTORICAL BUILDINGS IN THE CITY CENTRE (144 B–C4) (*ω b–c4*)

The centre of Macau is the pedestrian precinct *Largo de Senado*, Senate Square. With its uniform, perfectly restored buildings, it exudes a feeling of dignity even though a well-known American hamburger chain and similar shops have moved in and replaced local colour with standard international fare – as everywhere else. The most distinctive building on the south side is the *Leal Senado*, the 'loyal senate': the former town hall. You will not see this written on the building but Institute for Civil and Urban Affairs which has given rise to its new name of IACM Building. It was built at the end of the 18th century. Have a look at the distinguished panelled rooms on the upper floor: the Senate Library, which is open to the public, and the Council Hall. Painted tiles in the courtyards show historical views of the town. The rooms on the ground floor are used for temporary exhibitions. *Daily 9am–7pm*

If you take the small street on the right past the Leal Senado and walk uphill you will come to an ensemble of beautifully restored old buildings around the *Santo Agostinho Church*. Opposite this, lies the classicistic *Teatro Dom Pedro* from 1860; it is the oldest western-style theatre in the Far East.

When you return to Largo do Senado, you will see *São Domingos*, Macau's most beautiful Baroque church, at the northern end. It was built by the Dominicans in the 17th century and magnificently restored in 1996/97. The highlight is the main altar: the picture of the *Fátima* in the left side chapel is taken out of the church on a procession held on 13 May every year. The church museum is located in the bell tower (*daily 10am–6pm*).

LOW BUDGET

▸ *Casinos:* Entrance is free and visitors can see what is going on and breathe in the atmosphere. The most interesting are the large, new, bombastic buildings where there is always the most going on. Don't forget to take your passport with you!

▸ *Accommodation:* If you book in advance through the travel agencies in the *Shun Tak Centre* (132–133 C–D1) (*ω B10*) in Hong Kong, you will receive considerable reductions in the better hotels during the week.

▸ *San Va Hospedaria:* Stay in a romantic old building on Rua de Felicidade! Most of the 33 rooms are tiny (many without private bathrooms) and the walls are made of cardboard but you will only have to pay from HK$100 per night. *Rua da Felicidade 67 | tel. 28 57 37 01 | www. sanvahotel.com* (144 B4) (*ω b4*)

JARDIM DE LOU LIM IEOC
盧廉若公園 (145 D3) (*m d3*)

The most attractive park in Macau was established in the 19th century as the private garden of a Chinese merchant. He combined classic Chinese garden artistry

century. The first American-Chinese treaty was signed here in 1744. The goddess of compassion stands in the last hall of the central wing of the large complex whose individual small buildings are topped with colourfully decorated roofs in the typical

Jardim do Lou Lim Ieoc – miniature landscape and Macau's most beautiful park

with Macanese colonial architecture to create something very special. Visitors stroll through a miniature landscape of artificial mountains, bamboo groves and a goldfish pond with lotus flowers. Amateur musicians often perform in the pavilions. A museum on tea culture has been set up in a lovingly restored building on the edge of the garden. *Garden daily 6am–9pm, museum Tue–Sun 9am–7pm| Estrada de Adolfo Loureiro* 羅利老馬路

KUN IAM TONG 觀音堂
(145 D2–3) (*m d2–3*)

Guan Yin Hall, Macau's most important Buddhist temple, has its origins in the 17th

Cantonese style. Offerings are made to the recently deceased in two side halls. A passage on the eastern edge of the complex first leads out and then back to the rear temple garden. That is where the famous 'Lover's Tree' has been re-cultivated. The original of this strange tree with several trunks died in 1944. *Avenida do Coronel Mesquita* 美副將大馬路

LARGO DO LILAU 阿婆井前地 AND THE MANDARIN'S HOUSE 鄭家大屋
(144 B5) (*m b5*)

Atmospheric Lilau Square is bordered by an ensemble of restored houses. The small street going down the hill leads to the entrance of the impressive property once in the possession of a learned and wealthy Chinese family. Its most famous member was Zheng Guanying (1842–1921) an industrialist, writer and reformer. The once dilapidated buildings have been painstakingly renovated and visitors can now see some script tablets, furniture and fine carvings. *Fri–Tue 10am–6pm | free admission | Travessa de Antonio da Silva 龍頭左巷 10 | www.wh.mo/mandarinhouse*

LAS VEGAS HOTELS IN THE CENTRE
(144–145 C–D 4–5) (*ⅲ c–d 4–5*)

You can see it from far away: *Gran Lisboa's* crazy 258m (847ft) tower. This eye-catcher reminds some people of a Brazilian dancing girl with a feather boa and others of a lotus blossom. Moving pictures run across the surface of the balloon-like base at night. The next station is the *Wynn*. Every 15 minutes, colourful fountains of water start to play in front of its entrance. Once an hour, the 'Tree of Prosperity' grows up out of the floor in a round hall in the shopping centre while a chandelier with 21,000 crystals, illuminated by LEDs, descends from the ceiling. Half an hour later, the 'lucky dragon' floats up out of the mist.

The neighbouring *MGM Grand* thought up something completely different: an atrium with the façades of magnificent Lisbon houses. In all three cases – if you don't like kitsch, steer clear!

LIN FONG MIU 蓮峰廟
(145 D2) (*ⅲ d2*)

This temple was founded in 1592. The main figure in the first hall in the central wing is Tin Hau, the 'Heavenly Empress'. There are Buddhist figures in the second hall: compassionate Guan Yin in the centre, Weituo, the protector of the doctrine, on the left and Kshitigarbha, the ruler of hell, on the right. *Avenida do Almirante Lacerda 罅些喇提督大馬路*

MACAU MUSEUM 澳門博物館 AND FORTALEZA DO MONTE 大炮台 ★
(144 C3–4) (*ⅲ c3–4*)

Escalators whisk visitors up from the ruins of São Paulo to the City Museum that has found its home in the Mountain Fortress – the largest in Macau. It was built by the Jesuits between 1617 and 1626 and provides a lovely panoramic view. In 1622, a siege by the Dutch was warded off from here. *Platform daily 7am–sunset.*

● Macau Museum: A good collection of well-presented originals and models, together with audiovisual media and dioramas of the highest standard, breathes new life into old Macau – with façades of houses, shops and even the calls of street traders. *Tue–Sun 10am–6pm, last admission 5.30pm | entrance fee 15 Ptcs | www.macaumuseum.gov.mo*

MACAU TOWER 澳門旅遊塔 ☆
(144 B6) (*ⅲ b6*)

This 338m (1008ft)-high tower was erected on reclaimed land and, with its congress centre and new parliament building, makes a – not very convincing – contrast to the old city. But, the view form the top is magnificent. The adventurous climb up to the Skywalk in the open air – or make the deepest bungee jump on earth: 233m (765ft). *Daily 10am–9pm, revolving restaurant until 10pm | observation platform 120 Ptcs*

MA KOK MIU (A MA TEMPLE) 媽閣廟
(144 B5) (*ⅲ b5*)

The oldest temple in the city. The name Macau can be traced back the patron saint of seafarers who is worshiped here (*A Ma Gao*: A Ma Bay). The irregular, shady complex is made up of several small buildings on a steep slope above the sea. The main temple is at the bottom and there is a Guan Yin Temple higher up. *Largo do Pagode da Barra 媽閣廟前地*

Not a stroll for the faint-hearted: the skywalk on the Macau Tower

MUSEU DE ARTE 藝術博物館 AND HANDOVER GIFTS MUSEUM
澳門回歸賀禮陳列館
(145 E5) (*∅ e5*)

The MAM – the abbreviation used for Macao's art museum – is part of a culture centre and has a not very large permanent collection of Macanese paintings as well as space for temporary exhibitions. The Handover Gifts Museum adjoins it to the north. It stores the presents Macau received from all the other Chinese provinces when it 'returned' in 1999 – a show of Chinese splendour that is astonishing and frightening at the same time. *Tue–Sun 10am–7pm, entry until 6.30pm | entrance fee MAM 5 Ptcs, Handover Museum free | Avenida Xian Xing Hai* 冼星海大馬路 | *www.artmuseum.gov.mo | handover museum.iacm.gov.mo*

MUSEU MARÍTIMO 海事博物館
(144 A–B5) (*∅ a–b5*)

The splendid Maritime and Seafaring Museum is located opposite A Ma Temple (Ma Kok Miu). There are four sections: fishing in the South China Sea, sea travel and discoveries, marine biology, and harbour technology and hydrography. The exhibits – models, dioramas, aquariums, maritime maps, tools – have explanations in three languages. *Wed–Mon 10am–6pm, entry until 5.30pm | entrance fee 10 Ptcs, Sun 5 Ptcs | Largo do Pagode da Barra* 媽閣廟前地 | *www.museumaritimo.gov.mo*

PAWN HOUSE MUSEUM
典當業展示館 (144 B–C4) (*∅ b–c4*)

The fortress-like warehouse of pawned articles is very impressive and it is interesting to see how the boss kept his eye on the people working there. The house is part of the Culture Club with an excellent souvenir shop and tearoom. *Daily except 1st Mon in the month 10.30am–7pm | entrance fee 5 Ptcs | Avenida Almeida Ribero* 新馬路 396

PORTAS DO CERCO 關閘
(145 D1) (*∅ d1*)

This border gate to China was built in 1870 but today it is merely a monument in front of the gigantic checkpoint buildings. The date 'August 1849' on the front commem-

Symbol of the Mission: São Paulo

SÃO PAULO 大三巴牌坊
(144 C3–4) (🛇 c3–4)

The impressive façade of the cathedral that was destroyed by fire in 1835 is Macau's symbol and a cultural-historical monument of the first order. Japanese and Cantonese Christians erected it in the years 1620–27 to plans drawn up by an Italian Jesuit. This is a mission to Christianise the heathens in stone: the dove, as the symbol of the Holy Ghost, hovers at the top below the Cross; Jesus stands beneath it with Mary lower down who can be seen conquering a dragon further to the right; to the right of this, there is a *memento mori* in Chinese: 'If you think of death, you will not sin'. This is a counterpart to the inscription 'The devil leads man to sin' on the left next to the merchant ship. A subterranean museum at the end of the long vanished nave has exhibits of Christian art as well as the bones of Japanese and Vietnamese martyrs from the 17th century *(daily 9am–6pm)*.

TAIPA 氹仔
(146–147 A–D 1–2) (🛇 a–d 7–8)

The racetrack, university, airport and a satellite town are all located on the island that can be reached by crossing over a series of three bridges. A stroll through Taipa Village in the south is very pleasant. The traffic-free lanes are lined with two-storey houses, the main street Rua do Cunha – no cars here either – is well-known for its *pastelerias* (cake shops), cafés and restaurants. At the end, turn left and then right and go up the steps to reach the Carmelite Church built in the Classicist style in 1885. You now walk through a well cared-for park down to a body of water that was once part of the ocean from where you can see the hotel and casino palaces in Cotai. A row of five superbly restored villas on the shore, shaded by ancient trees, forms the *Taipa*

orates the murder of a governor of the city by rebellious Chinese and the subsequent retaliation campaign by the Portuguese. The inscription 'Honour your fatherland because it is watching you' warns those passing through the gate to remain faithful to Portugal. *At the northern edge*

PROTESTANT CEMETERY 基督教墳場 AND JARDIM LUIS DE CAMÕES 白鴿巢公園 (144 C3) (🛇 c3)

The shady Jardim Luis de Camões park recalls the great poet who lived in Macau for several years from 1558 and sang the praises of Portuguese conquests in his 'Os Lusiadas'.

The humble graveyard to the north-east of the park entrance is a history book in stone: plagues and pirates cut short the lives of merchants and sailors living here. *Praça Luís de Camões* 白鴿巢前地

House Museum. This is where you will be able to see how the 'better people' lived around 1900. The walk from here to *The Venetian* takes about 20 mins. *Busses 11, 15, 28A, 33*

FOOD & DRINK

Once you get away from the large hotels, the restaurants in Macau are much more easy-going and European than their bombastic competitors in Hong Kong – and cheaper too, especially when it comes to wine. The Macanese dishes are really unique – they are a combination of Portuguese and Cantonese cuisine with African chicken, Macau sole, codfish, shrimps and pigeon among the specialities.

ANTÓNIO 安東尼奧餐廳 (146 B2) (*∅ b8*)

António Coelho cooks at a level to satisfy gourmets in his simple 7-table restaurant in Taipa Village. The chef himself prepares many dishes in front of the guests at their table. *Rua dos Negociantes* 氹仔舊城區客商街 *3 | tel. 28 99 99 98 | www.antonio macau.com | Expensive*

INSIDER TIP ▶ CAFÉ OU MUN 澳門咖啡 (144 C4) (*∅ c4*)

Typical café-restaurant in a side street off Largo do Senado. Inexpensive set meals, Portuguese baked items and a wide range of sandwiches. *Travessa de São Domingos* 板樟堂巷 *12 | tel. 28 37 22 07 |*

CLUBE MILITAR 澳門陸軍俱樂部 (144 C4) (*∅ c4*)

There is no need to be afraid: the only things shooting around in this lovely old building are champagne corks. You will be served Portuguese cuisine in artistic surroundings. *Avenida da Praia Grande* 南灣大馬路 *795 | near Hotel Lisboa | tel. 28 71 40 00 | Moderate*

FERNANDOS 法蘭度餐廳 (147 D5) (*∅ d11*)

This fashionable restaurant lies hidden behind a bower of bougainvilleas at Hac Sa Beach. This is the place to enjoy spectacular seafood dishes. Terrace bar – no reservations! *Coloane* 路環黑沙海灘 *| Budget*

LITORAL 海灣餐廳 (144 B5) (*∅ b5*)

A top address for Macanese cuisine and one of the best places to try African Chicken. *Rua do Almirante Sergio* 河邊新街 *261A | near the Museu Marítimo | tel. 28 96 78 78 | Moderate*

INSIDER TIP ▶ NOODLE AND CONGEE CORNER 粥麵莊 (144 C4–5) (*∅ c4–5*)

In the casino – and still good and inexpensive? Hard to believe, but it's true. And there is more than just noodles and rice

FISH MASSAGE

OK, we won't repeat the worn out joke that you have to put your legs into a piranha aquarium in the ● *Fish Spa*. The small Garra Rufa fish that thoroughly clean your calves and create a pleasantly tickling effect while they are at work are completely harmless – and the results are amazing. Some people still feel the fish nibbling the following morning. *Shop 1209 | The Shoppes of Four Seasons (next to The Venetian) | Taipa | tel. 28 81 82 13* **(146 C3)** (*∅ c9*)

soup as the name seems to suggest. The open kitchen let's you see how soup is prepared with a single 10-foot-long noodle. *1st floor, Grand Lisboa* 新葡京酒店 | *tel. 28 28 38 38-77 55* | *Budget*

SHOPPING

The shopping arcades in the large hotels are full of international luxury articles. The *Rua de Nossa Senhora de Amparo* (144 C4) (*ᛗ c4*) and the adjacent streets is a good place for antiques and there is also a small flea market. *Artesanatos Fai Long (Rua São Paulo 33B)* sells first-rate painted porcelain figures made in the Shiwan ceramic centre.

ENTERTAINMENT

CENTRO CULTURAL 文化中心 (145 E5) (*ᛗ e5*)

It is impossible not to notice Macau's Cultural Centre with the floating roof of the theatre and concert building curving upwards. Artists from China and around the world make guest appearances here. *Avenida Xian Xing Hai* 冼星海大馬路 | *tel. 28 70 06 99* | *credit-card ticket sales tel. 28 40 05 55* | *www.ccm.gov.mo*

CIRQUE DU SOLEIL 太陽劇團 (146 C3) (*ᛗ c9*)

The Canadian circus enterprise presents its spectacular 'Zaia' show with a lot of thrilling acrobatics high up in the air at *The Venetian. Thu–Tue 8pm, Sat/Sun also at 5pm (starting times can vary)* | *tickets from 388 Ptcs* | *tel. 28 82 88 18* | *in Hong Kong tel. 63 33 66 60* | *www.cirquedusoleil. com*

THE HOUSE OF DANCING WATER 水舞間 ★ (146 C2) (*ᛗ c8*)

The most spectacular show in the eastern hemisphere. In an instant, the ring in the 2000-seat theatre changes into a pool of water out of which ships emerge and into which people disappear. The motorbike stunts in particular are really breathtaking. *Cotai, City of Dreams* | *Thu–Sun 5pm and 8pm, Mon 8pm (changes possible)* | *tickets from HK$480* | *ticket tel. 88 68 66 88* | *www.thehouseofdancingwater.com*

CASINOS

Gambling is Macau's main 'industry'. Most – and the largest – casinos are part of a hotel: see Cotai and Las Vegas above. *All open 24 hours* | *free admission*

DOCKS PUB ROW (145 D5) (*ᛗ d5*)

The destination of all night owls, with live music and dancing. *Avenida Dr. Sun Yat Sen near Avenida Sir Anders Ljungstedt*

WHERE TO STAY

Prices are always higher at weekends than on workdays. Hotels in Macau: *www. macautourism.gov.mo/en/info/accom modation.php.*

EAST ASIA 東亞酒店 (144 B4) (*ᛗ b4*)

Hotel with 98 rooms in the Old Town. The location is ideal for going on strolls to explore old Macau. *Rua da Madeira* 新埗頭街 1 | *tel. 28 92 24 33* | *Budget*

MANDARIN ORIENTAL 文華東方酒店 ✷ (145 D5) (*ᛗ d5*)

This hotel consciously resists trying to out-do the Las Vegas hotels and appearing just that little bit more bombastic. Instead, the Mandarin Oriental stresses refined elegance. There are wonderful views over the water from all bedrooms – and some bathrooms! *Avenida Dr Sun Yat Sen* 孫逸仙達馬路 | *tel. 88 05 88 88* | *www. mandarinoriental.com/macau* | *Expensive*

POUSADA DE MONG HÁ 望厦宾馆
(145 D2) (*d2*)

The romantic hotel run by the tourism college is the most highly-praised in the city: it has been lovingly decorated in Macanese style and the service and gastronomy is of the same excellent standard. The peaceful location on a green hill makes up for the less-than-ideal location. *Colina de Mong Há 望厦山 | tel. 28 51 52 22 | www.ift.edu.mo/pousada | Budget*

RIVIERA HOTEL 濠濕酒店
(144 B5) (*b5*)

Tranquil, sea views, inexpensive and only a short walk from the Old Town – these are the advantages of this 106-room hotel. *Rua Comendador Kou Ho Neng 高可寧紳士街 7–13 | tel. 28 33 99 55 | www.macauctshotel.com | Moderate*

THE WESTIN RESORT
威斯汀度假酒店
(147 D5) (*d11*)

208 rooms with views of the sea or beach, terrace, direct access to the golf course and a subtropical garden. The hotel has been classified a Green Hotel by Macau's environmental authorities. *Coloane, Estrada de Hac Sa 黑沙马路 1918 | tel. 28 87 11 11 | www.starwoodhotels.com | Moderate*

WYNN 永利澳门酒店
(145 C–D5) (*c–d5*)

Centrally located Las Vegas hotel with 1009 rooms. The suites in particular revel in luxury. Large casino, spacious spa area and really excellent dim sums in the **INSIDER TIP** Chinese Restaurant. *Rua Cidade de Sintra 仙德麗街 | tel. 28 88 99 66 | www.wynnmacau.com | Expensive*

Place your bets in the Grand Lisboa Casino: the Las Vegas of the east is in Macau

WALKING TOURS

The tours are marked in green in the street atlas, the pull-out map and on the back cover

1 EVERYDAY MIRACLES

Colourful life in Kowloon far away from the air-conditioned consumer world: house altars, chopping blocks, mahjong salons, fruit and vegetable markets, jade dealers and much more. Come in the late morning when all the shops are open and plan on 1½ hours – plus time for lunch.

The walk starts at the popular **Tin Hau Temple** → p. 44 in INSIDER TIP *Yau Ma Tei*. Some locals play cards and chess in the shade of the banyan trees in the forecourt, others idle away their time watching people go by or just reading the newspaper. Shops selling devotional objects such as figures of saints and house altars – a unique mixture in combination with others carrying household goods and hardware – line both sides of **Shanghai Street** that leads north. You will see a bizarre collection of Chinese fondue sets, scissors, gas lanterns, scales, lazy susan turntables, clay pots, chopping boards, wooden stools, incense and money for offerings, geomantic compasses and miniature stupas with space for Buddhist figures, and many other things on the street that is only a little more than 200m long. Ducks hang in a butcher's window

Photo: Statue Square

A kaleidoscope of Chinese and British elements: short tours through exotically colourful Hong Kong its history

and there are shrines dedicated to Guan Yu, the most beloved patron saint, on the back wall of many shops, usually with a bowl of fruit in front of the figure.

If you are walking on the west side of the street (right), change over to the other side at the junction with Man Ming Lane. The windows of the estate agent's on the corner (opposite the small park) are full of advertisements. The first number is usu-ally the size of the flat (in square feet) followed by the sales price in tens of thousands or the monthly rental written out fully in four figures.

Walk a block further along Shanghai St. towards the west until you reach the old halls of the wholesale fruit market. Later in the morning, things only get tidied up; the main business is done bright and early but the aroma and a few traders linger on for a while. The ancient buildings have been slated for demolition for some time, some are overgrown with plants and a real tree can be seen growing out of one of the gables.

Now, continue to the south. There are more metalware shops with articles for household and professional kitchens – some of them produced on the spot – on Reclamation Street. When you get to the shop at no. 181, you will ask yourself how they manage to get the gigantic steel coils in an out. There is a construction dating from 1923 at the northern end of Canton Road: the three-storey Yau Ma Tei Police Station with arcades on the ground floor. INSIDER TIP Café Kubrick (next to the art cinema) in the Prosperous Garden housing complex opposite the station serves food and drinks for the 'western' palate. Our walk now takes us further southwards to the Jade Market → p. 72. Go in through the second entrance (underneath the elevated highway) and take a look at the small booths on the right where professional scribes fill out tax declarations or help with applications for a taxi license. Some also provide Chinese-English translations. There is a row of shops selling minerals along Canton Road to the south. Here, you will be able to buy beautiful balls of rock crystal, fossils and pearls. The next stop (to the left, through Pak Hoi St.) is the Reclamation Street Fruit and Vegetable Market – a whole symphony of harmonious aromas with some fishy dissonances.

After you have looked around, return to Pak Hoi St. and go one street further on to the east as far as Shanghai Street. Have a look at house no. 189 with jade and wooden carvings, no. 185 where incense is sold and the cookhouse at no. 183. Cross the street – there is a typical pawnshop (with an enormously high counter and barred windows) at no. 178 on the

corner of Saigon St. and snake soup is served at no. 164 throughout the year. Go back and turn right onto Saigon Street. Your eyes will be drawn to the two large tin kettles in the herbal chemist's on the next corner with a photograph of the firm's owner hanging above them. Cups of medicinal tea will have been brewed just waiting to be tasted.

Cross Temple Street → p. 71, 79; during the day, you will find it hard to believe that there is so much activity here at night. Immediately on the left, mahjong games are sold. A magnificent large mahjong salon – its façade covered in yellow marble – follows at nos. 70–72 Woosung Street with another one opposite it. Stay on Woosung St. and walk south until you reach the cookhouse at no. 97; this is where you can have a lunch of delicious rice soup and other dishes for next to nothing.

2 TRACES OF HISTORY

This 90-minute walk will take you to the most important sites of the early colonial period that have been preserved in the centre.
Start out in Hong Kong's 'front room' Statue Square → p. 28 where you will see an ugly skyscraper opposite the elegant Mandarin Oriental Hotel → p. 84. It is the seat of the time-honoured Hong Kong Club. The cenotaph in front of it was erected in 1919 and now serves to remember those who fell in the two World Wars. Cross Charter Road. Until well into the 1950s, it ran along the shore and was itself created around 1900 on reclaimed land. Statue Square, where you are now standing, was originally named after the statue of Queen Victoria that was melted down by the Japanese in World War II. The statue near the southeast corner shows

Sir Thomas Jackson (1841–1915), one of the heads of the Hong Kong and Shanghai Bank. Its headquarters and those of two other Hong Kong financial institutes look down on you from above: on the right,

Street. The beautiful wide flight of steps at its southern end was laid out in 1880 and is decorated with four gas lanterns. This leads to Ice House Street named after the ice from the USA that was stored here in

In the shadow of the glass palaces: St John's Cathedral, the main Anglican church in Hong Kong

the Standard Chartered Bank, in the centre the HSBC Main Building → p. 32 and the Bank of China → p. 29 soaring up like a gigantic geometrical sculpture behind the HSBC's old offices. The old domed building on the (left) east side of the square is the Legco Building → p. 33 with Chater Garden, opened in 1978, behind it. Until that time, one of the most valuable pieces of land in the city was taken up by the Cricket Club pitches.

Walk up Garden Road until you reach St John's Cathedral → p. 35. If you leave the church through the main entrance, you will catch sight of the French Mission Building → p. 31 – today, the seat of the Supreme Court – on the right.

Now follow Battery Path, shaded by old trees, on the left until you reach Duddell

summer to be used by the dairy at 2 Lower Albert Road. Today, this is the location of the foreign correspondents' club. The neighbouring building (home of the Fringe Culture Club → p. 79) was built in the same style in 1913. The back of the building, on Wyndham Street, is even more impressive than its façade. The art and antique dealers' district starts on the flat section of Wyndham St. Now you are nor far away from Hong Kong's largest complex of colonial buildings: the Central Police Station → p. 30 complete with adjoining prison. Pottinger Street on the right still has its old road surface.

The impressive portal of the Magistrates' Building, built in 1914, dominates Arbuthnot Road that begins on the side of the Police Station. Our next destination is Government House. This former seat of the Governor dates back to 1855 but has been enlarged many times since. For example, the tower is the work of the Japanese occupying forces in World War II. Hong Kong's chief administrator made a fuss about taking up his official residence here until 2006 although the last Governor, Chris Patten, had already vacated the premises on 30 June, 1997.

Where the steps meet Garden Rd. you will see a white building: The Helena May, a club for women dating from 1916. The Peak Tram departs from the lower floor of the next skyscraper up the hill. Go under the elevated highway until you reach Hong Kong Park → p. 32, follow the road to the left and then the signs to Flagstaff House, erected 1844–46 as the residence of the captain of the garrison; it is the oldest colonial building left in the city.

3 GINSENG, ART AND SHARKS' FINS

This tour (of at least 2 hours) combines ginseng and dried-fish wholesalers with the art business on Cat St. and Hollywood Row and a few temples. Note: shops are closed in the morning and on Sundays and public holidays.

After you leave the Sheung Wan MTR station through exit A1, turn right and right again onto Man Wa Lane where you will find a row of small stands run by people who carve seal stamps and print visiting cards. Continue until you reach Bonham Strand. Just past the next crossing, you will see the first of many wholesalers of dried mushrooms, ginseng and swallows' nests. The nests are packed in round transparent plastic containers. There is a typical tea shop at nos. 105–107 that also sells 'brick tea': tea leaves pressed to form blocks or discs. No. 24, a household shop, still mainly sells a traditional range of articles. Turn right towards the Western Market from 1906; this is the stronghold of the fabric dealers (on the upper floor). Two streets further south, there are two floors of groceries in the Sheung Wan Market followed by a cookhouse market.

Up a few steps (Tung St.) and you have arrived at Cat Street → p. 70 where bric-a-brac and fakes are sold alongside first-rate antiques. Take the steps down at the eastern end of Cat St. and have a break in Lok Cha Tea Shop → p. 73. The next highlight is the Man Mo Temple → p. 33. Hollywood Road → p. 70 towards the west is a single, gigantic art gallery. Then walk through Upper Station St. to Kwun Yum Tong Temple (Guan Yin Hall) with golden carvings hanging in front of the entrance. There is another Guan Yin hall down the steps immediately on the right; this one has 60 gold-plated gods of the years on the left wall and a wheel of fortune. You can see cranes sitting in a pine tree on the tile picture to the right of the steps – in China, both symbolise the same thing: longevity. Now go to the right and the junction with Possession Street. Its name reminds one that it was here that the British first raised the Union Jack on 26 January, 1841.

It's time for a rest and Hollywood Park is a good place for this. There is another group of shops selling dried food, herbs and ginseng on the right-hand side of Queen's Road West. The other side of the street is more interested in the world beyond: here, you can buy everything from sports shoes to mobile telephones made of paper to offer your ancestors. After you reach house no. 181, go down to Des Voeux Road West and then turn right. Here, dried fish wholesalers attack all of your sensory organs with their codfish, shrimps, mussels, seahorses, fish lips, etc. Some shops (no. 104, for example) also

Fresh food for Hong Kong's gourmets: groceries at Sheung Wan Market

have sharks' fins; dried, they can cost much more than HK$10,000 per kilo. You can reach the underground through Bonham Strand West.

4 THE PEAK FROM THE OTHER SIDE

🚶 **Instead of queuing up endlessly to wait for the Peak Tram on a sunny weekend, you can hike up shady mountain paths: through Pok Fu Lam Country Park. It takes about one hour; the total time including the bus trip there is around 90 minutes. Take something to drink with you.**

You set out for 🙂 Pok Fu Lam Country Park by bus lines 7 or 91 from Central (e.g. from the bus station near the ferry docks (in front of Tower 2 of the International Finance Centre). When the view to the right from the bus no long shows dense construction but becomes greener, you should start to pay attention – even more so when you see the Ebenezer School (on the right, large sign). Around 300m after this, the bus passes Woodbury Court (also on the right, also large sign) and you should press the button and get out at the Pok Fu Lam Reservoir Road stop (on a hilltop). The rest is easy: go up the side street from the bus stop and you will see the first information signs after around 250m. The route is signposted after that, although there are a few alternatives. The shortest path is along the closed road – you can't get lost. There are pavilions and benches for having a break along the way and boards with information on the flora and fauna in the area.

TRAVEL WITH KIDS

Hong Kong is probably not really one of the first destinations tourists think of visiting with children – but just take a look: it is more interesting for the young ones than you may expect! It starts with the parks: the Avarium in Hong Kong Park, the bird pond in Kowloon Park and the zoo are all pleasant places to visit, and educational too, and no admission is charged to any of them. There is even a large open-air swimming pool at the northern end of Kowloon Park.

The Science Museum is also a good choice – especially if the weather is bad, as the many young visitors go to prove. The sophisticated presentation technology in the Museum of History makes it especially interesting for school children *(Entrance fee for pupils and students: Science Museum HK$12.50 | Museum of History HK$5 | identification required)*.

Ocean Park: although the area after the entrance is no longer officially called *Kid's World*, the most important activities for children can still be found there – and provide a great variety of entertainment and education *(entrance fee for children from 3–11, HK$125)*.

APE COLONY AT THE SHEK LEI PUI RESERVOIR 石梨貝水庫
(139 D3) (*Ⓜ 0*)

Rhesus monkeys which now live on the northern edge of Kowloon used to be common in Hong Kong – but most of them had been wiped out by the middle of the 20th century. It is possible that all the monkeys frolicking around between the bus stop and reservoir are descendants of some who managed to escape their fate. Take the ban on feeding them seriously: the animals can become aggressive. This little excursion – a bus trip and short walk – takes about 2 hours. *Bus 81 from MTR Yau Ma Tei/exit A1 to Shek Lei Pui Reservoir*

DISNEYLAND 迪士尼樂園
(138 C4) (*Ⓜ 0*)

Hong Kong is really proud to have the first Asian Disneyland outside Japan. The park is divided into four sections of amazement and adventure: *Main St. USA* takes visitors back to around 1900 with a street theatre, a parade and a lot of music; in *Adventureland* visitors take a ride on a raft through the jungle to Tarzan's tree house and take part in the Lion King's Festival;

The jungle of skyscrapers offers more for children than you possibly thought – and some attractions are even free

Mickey Mouse is the guide through a fairy-tale world of roundabouts and Sleeping Beauty's Castle in *Fantasyland*, while children and adults will marvel at the peaceful and exciting future in *Tomorrowland*. *Daily 10.30am–8.30pm, during the summer holidays 10am–8.30pm | entrance fee HK$350, children (3–11) HK$250, senior citizens (over 65) HK$170 | limited number of tickets, advance bookings: tel. 183 08 30 or online | www.hongkongdisneyland. com | MTR Disneyland Resort*

ICE SKATING AT CITY PLAZA
太古城中心冰上皇宮 (U D3) (𝄞 0)
No, it's is not a joke! Hong Kong's largest shopping centre, City Plaza, even has an ice-skating rink. You can rent skates there. *Mon–Fri 9.30am–10pm, Sat 12.30–10pm, Sun 12.30–6.30 pm | entrance fee from HK$45 (weekday mornings) | www.icepalace.com.hk | MTR Tai Koo, exit E1*

SNOOPY'S WORLD 史諾比開心世界
(139 D3) (𝄞 0)
Charlie Brown is here and so are Schroeder, Linus, Lucy, Woodstock, and of course Charlie's philosophical beagle, as well as all the other figures from the comic series – more than 60 in all. *Daily 10am–8pm | admission free | Sha Tin New Town Plaza 新城市廣場 | Phase One, Level 3 | Sha Tin station, exit A*

WITH CHILDREN IN MACAU
The *Science Center (daily 10am–6pm, last entrance 5.30pm | entrance fee 25 Ptcs, 2–11 years of age 15 Ptcs | opposite the Culture Centre)* (145 E5) (𝄞 e5) focuses especially on its young visitors. *Kid's City (daily 10.30am–9.30pm | Hard Rock Hotel, Level 2 | City of Dreams)* (146 C2) (𝄞 c8) offers a lot of fun for children from 2 to 12. There are rules though: long sleeves, trousers and socks.

FESTIVALS & EVENTS

PUBLIC HOLIDAYS

1 Jan New Year's Day; **Chinese New Year** (three days); **Ching Ming Festival**; **Good Friday to Easter Monday**; **Dragon Boat Festival**; **1 July** Foundation of SAR Hong Kong; **2 July**; **3rd Monday in August** Liberation Day; **Day after Mid-Autumn Festival**; **Chung Yeung Festival**; **25/26 Dec** Christmas

CHINESE FESTIVALS

Roman numerals = lunar months

1 I CHINESE NEW YEAR
(10 Feb, 2013/31 Jan, 2014) This festival is just as important for Chinese families as Christmas is for us. Most shops close for 2 days or longer. The decorations are really spectacular and there is a magnificent flower market in Victoria Park before the festival. There is a New Year's Parade on the 2nd day and fireworks over the harbour in the evening. It is forbidden to let of fireworks. The festival season ends on the 15th day with the lantern festival to celebrate the first full moon.

4 OR 5 APRIL: CHING MING FESTIVAL
Festival to commemorate the dead: families sweep the graves of their ancestors and bring offerings of food and drink.

23 III BIRTHDAY OF TIN HAU
(2 May 2013 and 22 April 2014) decorated ships go to Tin Hau Temple on the **INSIDER TIP** goddess' birthday. There, the seafarers make sacrifices to their patron saint, enjoy themselves with lion dances and have their boats' shrines blessed for the coming year *(139 E4) (\u00d8 0)*. *Special ferries from North Point (135 F1) (\u00d8 0)*.

8 IV BIRTHDAY OF TAM KUNG AND BUDDHA
(17 May 2013, 6 May 2014) Celebrations for Tam Kung, the Ruler of the Weather, in his main temple in Shau Kei Wan *(MTR Shau Kei Wan, north end of Main St.) (U E3) (\u00d8 0)*. This is also the day when the statues of Buddha in temples are washed.

IV MONTH: BUN FESTIVAL IN CHEUNG CHAU
The **INSIDER TIP** Bun Festival in honour of the God of the North (the main god of

Colourful birthday celebrations for the gods, exciting dragon boat races, the mystery of incense in autumn

the island) lasts 3 days. The exact date is determined by an oracle. The procession is absolutely spectacular; colourfully costumed children, supported by hidden frames, seem to float on the hands of other children. Pink buns which bring good luck are hung from three 20m (66ft)-high towers and distributed by the priests on the last evening. (138 B–C5) (⌂ 0)

5 V DRAGON BOAT FESTIVAL (TUEN NG FESTIVAL)

(12 June 2013, 2 June 2014) People eat sticky rice and organise spectacular dragon boat races. The international races in Sha Tin are held one or two weeks later.

15 VIII MID-AUTUMN FESTIVAL (MOON FESTIVAL)

(19 Sept 2013, 8 Sept 2014) Coloured lanterns glow, people look at the moon and eat rich moon cakes. The dances by the

INSIDER TIP ▶ fire dragons made of glowing incense sticks that wind their way through the lanes near Wun Sha Street are an unforgettable sight. (135 E4) (⌂ H12)

9 IX DOUBLE NINE (CHUNG YEUNG FESTIVAL)

(13 Oct 2013, 2 Oct 2014) Hong Kongers make offerings at the graves and excursions into the surrounding hills.

FESTIVALS & SPORTS

FEBRUARY/MARCH

▶ *Arts Festival:* varied programme with performances by top artists from around the world. Music, ballet and theatre. *www.hk.artsfestival.org*

NOVEMBER

▶ *Macau Grand Prix:* Classic car race. *www.macau.grandprix.gov.mo*

LINKS, BLOGS, APPS & MORE

LINKS

▶ m.discoverhongkong.com Free access to the tourism sites of the Hong Kong Tourism Board at the 7000 hotspots of the provider PCCW

▶ www.hongkongextras.com A non-commercial English guide with a mass of detailed information on construction projects, changes to public transport connections, ferry fares, etc.

▶ gohongkong.about.com Another independent English travel guide; less detailed but more focused on recommendations and – a big plus – Macau is also included

▶ www.openrice.com/english Hong Kong's most comprehensive online gourmet guide with guest reviews, photos, recipes and search function (key words, districts)

▶ www.hongkonghustle.com Art, parties, fashion, music; in short, this is where you can find out about the lifestyle of the metropolis

BLOGS

▶ www.hkdigit.net Photo-blog in English, a variety of subjects seen from the Hong Kong perspective

▶ http://blog.yahoo.com/deli-prince-club/articles/page/1 Gourmet blog with the latest restaurant tips! English texts (short and to the point), Chinese signs (useful in taxis). Unfortunately, not much on Macau

▶ http://directory.bestblogs.asia/hong-kong-blog List of Hong Kong blogs on a variety of subjects

▶ www.blogmacau.info News from the casino town

▶ toiletbar.blogspot.com Humorous reports by Larry Feign, who lives in a traffic-free village on Lantau with his wife; a completely different angle on Hong Kong

Regardless of whether you are still preparing your trip or already in Cape Town: these addresses will provide you with more information, videos and networks to make your holiday even more enjoyable

▶ www.youtube.com/user/HongKong Reality channel of the Hong Kong Tourism Board with around 30 well-made short films

▶ www.tripfilms.com/Tourism-l62489-Hong_Kong-Travel_Videos.html Mainly amateur videos; those made by heavyGFilms give an insight into restaurants and their kitchens

▶ www.tripfilms.com/search.sdo?keywords=Macau&x=0&y=0 A small selection of videos on Macau – including a gondola ride in *The Venetian* casino palace

▶ www.youtube.com/watch?v=CX9nmUDkmrY&NR=1 Mainly videos of bungee jumps from the Macau Tower; this one of a jump at night is probably the most spectacular

▶ www.goandroam.com/webcams/china/hk Collection of Hong Kong webcams with photos changing every 15 minutes; with a Macau link

▶ http://traffic.td.gov.hk/SwitchCenter.do Webcam photos of many streets

▶ HKTB Mobile Guides An entire collection of Hong Kong apps commissioned by the Hong Kong Tourism Board

▶ KMB Bilingual app from Kowloon Motor Bus for your iPhone

▶ www.flickr.com/groups/hongkong Hong Kong forum for hobby photographers – useful tips and wonderful pictures

▶ twitoaster.com/country-hk The ultimate overview of twitterers in Hong Kong

▶ http://community.justlanded.com/en/Hong-Kong A comprehensive forum aimed at people who intend to stay in Hong Kong for a lengthy period

▶ http://forum.chinaorbit.com Forum on all things Chinese including Hong Kong and Macau

TRAVEL TIPS

ARRIVAL (HONG KONG)

There are a great number of flights to Hong Kong; either direct from London or with stopovers. Compare the price of flights offered by major airlines on the Internet. As a rule, a nonstop flight from Europe takes around 12 hours. All planes land at Chek Lap Kok Airport. If you do not have a pressing engagement, you should take one of the **INSIDER TIP** Airport Express buses to the inner city as they travel over three elevated bridges with spectacular views. In addition, it is possible to reach many destinations without having to change.

Airport Express: The trip to the terminus in Central (133 E2) (*∅ C11*) costs HK$100, to the Kowloon stop HK$90 (travel time 23 and 19 minutes respectively). Buses depart from the train stations to the larger hotels. Onward travel by underground (change at Tsing Yi and Hong Kong stops) and special shuttle buses that travel on several routes to around 50 hotels from the Kowloon and Hong Kong stations is free of charge.

Buses: Air-conditioned Airbuses travel directly to several hotels. Line 11A makes the journey via Causeway Bay to North Point in 70 minutes (HK$40), line A21 to Kowloon Station (MTR Hung Hom, HK$33, 65 minutes). The exact fare has to be inserted when you get on. In addition, comfortable hotel buses connect the airport with several major hotels; tickets are available at counters C07 and C08 in Terminal 2.

Taxis: Green cabs only drive in the New Territories; blue ones on Lantau. Count on paying HK$350 to reach Central and Causeway Bay and HK$280 for Tsim Sha Tsui (incl. bridge and tunnel fees).

Trains arriving directly from China end at the Kowloon/Hung Hom station (131 E4) (*∅ F–G8*), where passport and customs control takes place. From there, it is only a 5-minute taxi ride to the Kowloon hotels and 5–15 minutes to the island. The tunnel buses that stop at the railway station are a much cheaper way of reaching the island but they are often overcrowded and hardly practical if you have much luggage with you.

Cruise liners dock at Ocean terminal (130 B6) (*∅ D9*); ferries from China at the China Ferry Terminal (130 B5) (*∅ D8–9*). Taxis and buses leave from the lower floor.

ARRIVAL (MACAU)

There are no direct flights to Macau from Europe. You can reach Macau

RESPONSIBLE TRAVEL

It doesn't take a lot to be environmentally friendly whilst travelling. Don't just think about your carbon footprint whilst flying to and from your holiday destination but also about how you can protect nature and culture abroad. As a tourist it is especially important to respect nature, look out for local products, cycle instead of driving, save water and much more. If you would like to find out more about eco-tourism please visit: *www.ecotourism.org*

From arrival to weather

Holiday from start to finish: the most important addresses and information for your Hong Kong and Macau trip

from the airport in Hong Kong without actually entering the SAR by using the Turbojet and Cotai Jet services. Those in a real hurry can take a helicopter. *(9am–11pm every 30 mins. | flying time 15 mins. | HK$2900 one way | Hongkong tel. 2018 98 98, Macau tel. 28 72 72 88 | www.sky shuttlehk.com). Departure and landing at the ferry terminals but not from China Ferry Terminal and Taipa Temporary Terminal.*

Jet-propelled catamarans and hover-craft operated by the Turbojet Shipping Company depart round the clock from Macau Ferry Terminal (132–133 C–D1) (m B10). *7am–midnight, every 15 mins. | travel time 60 mins. | HK$134 from Hong Kong, 142 Ptcs/HK$ from Macau (one way economy fare, incl. exit fee| information: Hong Kong tel. 28 59 33 33, Macau tel. 87 90 36 28.* There are higher fares at weekends and at night and an extra charge for large pieces of luggage (more than 10kg).

First Ferry *(www.nwf.com.hk)* departs from the China Ferry Terminal (130 B5) (m D8–9) every 30 mins. and the prices for the journey are similar.

A third alternative is Cotai Jet *(www.cotaijet.com.mo)* to the so-called Taipa Temporary Terminal; from there, it is not very far to the Las Vegas casinos in Cotai. Departures from the Macau Ferry Terminal every 30 mins. between 9am–11pm; every hour or every 2 hours at other times. The prices are the same as with Turbojet.

Bookings for the ferries can be made at the docks, in travel agencies and some underground stations, as well as on the Internet. During the week, there are usually spaces free but a reservation is advisable at the weekend. It is not worth pay-

BUDGETING

Beer, wine	£3.70/$6	for a draught beer or glass of wine
Lunch	£2.90/$4.50	for Chinese noodle soup
Dinner	£13–20/$20–30	in an average standard Chinese restaurant
Peak Tram	£3.30/$5.20	for a return trip to The Peak
Bus fare	23p/¢50	in the city in Macau
Casino show	£40/$65	in a casino theatre in Macau

ing the additional money for a first-class ticket.

In Macau, buses 3, 3A and 10A depart from the airport (145 E3–4) (m e3–4) for the centre and pass several hotels on the way. The larger hotels and casino hotel complexes on Cotai provide free shuttle buses. There are similar connections to the airport. Taxis from the ferry landing to the centre cost around 25 Ptcs.

BANKS & CURRENCY EXCHANGE

There are several exchange offices on arrival level 5 at the airport | daily 7am–10.30pm The most convenient way to get cash is from a dispenser using your bank card. Charges vary depending on your bank or credit card. If you change money or cash travellers' cheques elsewhere, the fees can be higher than the difference in the exchange rate. You can pay with your credit card in all hotels and most restaurants.

CLIMATE, WHEN TO GO

The ideal period is between the middle of Oct and the end of Dec when it is almost always warm and dry. The weather can be damp and chilly in Feb and March. Summers are muggy and hot. The typhoon season is Aug–Oct; when signal level 8 is sounded, schools, offices and shops close, ferries stop running, followed a little later by bus and rail transport.

COMPLAINTS

The Consumer Council can help if you feel that you have been cheated shopping: *tel. 29 29 22 22 | www.consumer.org.hk*

CUSTOMS

1 litre of spirits (30+% alcohol content) and 19 cigarettes can be imported duty free into Hong Kong. In Macau, this is 1 litre of wine or spirits (30% alcohol content), 1 litre of spirits with a higher alcoholic content and 200 cigarettes. When you return to the EU, the same tax-exemption limit for cigarettes applies as it does in Macau and, in addition, 1 litre of sprits above 22% or 2 litres with less alcohol, as well as 4 litres of wine. For allowances, *see: www.hmrc.gov.uk/customs/arriving/arrivingnoneu.htm*

ELECTRICITY

The power supply in Hong Kong and Macau is the same as in Europe: 220V. Hong Kong uses the British three-pin rectangular blade plug although there are other plug variations too. If your hotel does not have multiple wall sockets, they will usually provide adapters (also available cheaply from electrical shops).

EMBASSIES & CONSULATES

BRITISH CONSULATE-GENERAL
1 Supreme Court Road | Hong Kong | tel. +852 29 01 30 00 | ukinhongkong.fco.gov.uk/en/

CONSULATE GENERAL OF THE UNITED STATES OF AMERICA
26 Garden Road | Hong Kong | tel: +852 25 23 90 11 | hongkong.usconsulate.gov/contact.html

CONSULATE GENERAL OF CANADA
12th–14th Floor | One Exchange Square | Hong Kong | tel. +852 37 19 47 00 | www.canadainternational.gc.ca/hong_kong

EMERGENCY SERVICES

Fire Brigade, Ambulance, Assault: tel. 999 (without coins)
Police (for tourists; also for taxi complaints): tel. 23 27 71 77

EVENT INFORMATION

Advance information is available at *www.discoverhongkong.com* ('Events & Festivals', with interactive calendar). Information for partygoers and pub crawlers is provided by *www.bcmagazine.net*. The weekly 'HK Magazine' can be picked up in many places free of charge. Flyers on cultural events are available at the Cultural Centre and in City Hall.

HEALTH

No vaccinations are prescribed for Hong Kong. You should not drink large quantities of tap water that has not been boiled. The following hospitals have 24-hour emergency services: *Queen Mary Hospital | 102 Pokfulam Rd. | Hong Kong Island | tel. 28 55 38 38* (U A4) (*∭ 0*) and *Queen Elizabeth Hospital | 30 Gascoigne Rd. | Kowloon | tel. 29 58 88 88* (131 D3) (*∭ E–F7*). *St John Ambulance* (free ambulance service): on the island *tel. 25 76 65 55* | Kowloon *tel. 27 13 55 55* | New Territories *tel. 26 39 25 55*.

The consulate can provide information on English-speaking doctors. Medication is provided directly by doctors and hospitals. Medicine can also be purchased at some *Watson's* branches, e.g. *Melbourne Plaza | 33 Queen's Rd. Central* (133 D3) (*∭ C11*), *11 Cameron Rd.* (130 C5) (*∭ E9*).

IMMIGRATION

Hong Kong has a separate immigration system from that of mainland China and most visitors do not need to obtain visas in advance. Full British citizens with a valid passport can stay for up to 180 days visa-freee as visitors; citizens from British Overseas Territories, members of all EU countries, the USA and Canada for up to 90 days. You will also need your passport if you intend to travel between Hong Kong and Macau. Normally, formalities are handled quickly but you will have to fill out a small form. You should be at the departure counter 15 minutes before your ferry (or helicopter) leaves. A visa is still required to enter mainland China from Hong Kong.

INFORMATION BEFORE THE TRIP

HONG KONG TOURIST BOARD (HKTB)
www.discoverhongkong.com/eng/index.html

MACAU GOVERNMENT TOURIST OFFICE
www.macautourism.gov.mo

INFORMATION IN HONG KONG

HONG KONG TOURISM BOARD (HKTB)
– *Visitor tel. 25 08 12 34 | daily 9am–6pm*
– *Visitor Information:*
– *at the airport (only for arriving passengers)*
– *at the Star Ferry Dock | Kowloon | daily 8am–8pm* (130 C6) (*∭ E9*)
– *at the Peak Piazza (between the Peak Tower and Peak Galleria) | daily 9am–9pm* (132 C5) (*∭ B13*)

MACAU TOURIST INFORMATION BUREAU
– *Shop 336–337, Shun Tak Centre | 200 Connaught Rd. Central | tel. 28 57 22 87 | daily 9am–10pm* (132–133 C–D 1–2) (*∭ B10*)
– *Hong Kong International Airport | counter A06, arrival level 5, terminal 1* (0) (*∭ 0*)

ACCOMMODATION SERVICE
At the airport (only for arriving passengers)

INFORMATION IN MACAU

MACAU GOVERNMENT TOURIST OFFICE
– *Largo do Senado 9 | daily 9am–6pm | tel. 83 97 11 20* (144 C4) (*∭ c4*)
– *additional counters (some with accommodation service) in the Macau Ferry Terminal* (145 E3–4) (*∭ e3–4*), *Taipa Ferry Terminal* (147 D1) (*∭ d7*), *at the airport* (147 D1–2) (*∭ d7–8*) *and other locations*
– *Visitor tel. 28 33 30 00*

INTERNET CAFÉS & WI-FI

All better hotels and shopping centres provide wireless internet access (Wi-Fi); however, you will usually have to pay extra for this service. Internet terminals that can be used free of charge can be found on the second floor of the *China Hong Kong City (China Ferry Terminal)* (130 B5) (*Ø D–E8*). Internet access is free in most government buildings including the foyer of *City Hall* (133 E3) (*Ø D11*).

All government hotspots are listed under *www.gov.hk/en/theme/wifi/location/index.htm,* others at *www.ofta.gov.hk/en/consumer_interest/main.html* (Menu: 'Search for Registered Wi-Fi Access Points'). You will be able to surf the net while drinking coffee in the branches of *Pacific Coffee,* e.g. *International Finance Centre, level 1, shop 1022* (133 E2) (*Ø C11*) and *132 Nathan Rd.* (130 C4) (*Ø E8*).

OPENING HOURS

The shops in Tsim Sha Tsui and Causeway Bay are usually open from 10am–9pm, some until 10pm, also at weekends; in Central only until around 7.30pm. Many specialist shops remain closed on Sunday. The opening hours in Macau are similar. The shops in the arcades in the casino palaces all close before 11pm.

PHONE & MOBILE PHONE

Your mobile phone will connect automatically to the Hong Kong network. Using your mobile to telephone home is not all that expensive but it can cost a lot to be called. If you stay in Hong Kong for a longer period of time, it might be worthwhile buying a local SIM card or a worldwide prepaid card such as *Travelsim (new.travelsimshop.com)*. Phonecards, sold by the *Circle K* and *7-Eleven* chains (the shops are often open at night) are the cheapest way to call internationally for those travelling without a mobile phone. Telephoning from your hotel room is frequently costly. Calls within Hong Kong's fixed-line network are free but cost HK\$1 from a payphone. The international dialing code to the UK is *0044*, US/Canada *001*. The code for Hong Kong is *00852*, for Macau *00853*.

POST

Hong Kong Island: main post office near the Star Ferry (133 E2) (*Ø C11*) | *Mon–Sat 8am–6pm, Sun 9am–5pm; Tsim Sha Tsui: 10 Middle Rd.* (130 C5–6) (*Ø E9*) | *Mon–Sat 9am–6pm, Sun 9am–2pm*

PRICES & CURRENCY

The Hong Kong dollar, abbreviated here as HK\$, is pegged to the US dollar with a range of 7.75 to 7.85 (US\$1 = HK\$7.75–7.85) and the exchange rate to other currencies fluctuates accordingly. The bank notes are issued by three different banks, have the same size but different designs. Prices in Macau (calculated in Patacas – Ptcs) are generally somewhat lower than in Hong Kong. You can pay with Hong Kong currency in Macau (the rate is 1:1) but make sure you get your change in dollars.

PUBLIC TRANSPORT

IN HONG KONG

Mass Transit Railway: MTR for short, is the name of Hong Kong's underground and suburban railway company. It runs services on ten lines. A single ticket from a machine costs from HK\$3.50 (usually, at least HK\$4). It is only permitted to go to the two border stations Lo Wu and Lok Ma Chau with travel documents.

Buses: There are several companies. The lines through the harbour tunnels are noted with red, three-digit numbers. Folders issued by the Hong Kong Tourism Board provide information on the most important lines. You have to insert the exact fare (usually HK$4–10) when you get on a bus. A display shows the name of the next stop in some buses. *www.mtr.com.hk*

Services stop at around midnight but some buses run throughout the night. Minibuses with green stripes (maxi cabs) operate like the big buses but those with red stripes stop wherever needed, like a taxi – without any knowledge of Cantonese and the route, you will never end up where you want to go.

Trams: Very inexpensive. You pay when you get off (HK$2.30, no change). Stations are not called out.

Light Rail Transit: A modern tram in the west of the New Territories.

Peak Tram: Buy a return ticket when you get on if you don't plan to walk down the hill (single fare HK$28, return HK$40). You will have a better view if you sit on the right. There is no need to buy the expensive *Peak Tram Sky Pass* including the fee for the observation terrace that, in no way, offers the best panoramic view.

Ferries: The last Star Ferry sails at 11.30pm. Most ferries to the islands depart from the piers in Central (133 D–E 1–2) (🕮 C10–11). The tariffs are higher at the weekend. The expensive express ferries are not especially attractive for tourists. *Information:* Ferries to Lantau (Mui Wo) and Cheung Chau tel. 21318181, Lamma Island tel. 28156063, Tolo Harbour tel. 22722022

The magic word for comfortable travel in Hong Kong is the INSIDER TIP *Octopus-Card.* It costs HK$100 – that is the stored credit – plus HK$50 deposit, is valid in

CURRENCY CONVERTER

£	HKD	HKD	£
1	12.5	10	0.80
3	23	30	2.4
5	63	50	4
13	163	130	10.4
40	500	400	32
75	940	750	60
120	1500	1200	96
250	3140	2500	200
500	6280	5000	400

$	HKD	HKD	$
1	8	10	1.25
3	23.5	30	2.50
5	39	50	6.3
13	102	130	16.3
40	315	400	50
75	590	750	94
120	940	1200	150
250	1965	2500	313
500	3930	5000	625

For current exchange rates see www.xe.com

most means of public transport and can be used as soon as you leave the airport. You can return it at the airport (or in underground stations) and any credit remaining plus the deposit in cash will be refunded in cash (minus a small service charge). When you go through a barrier (e.g. in an MTR station) or get on a bus, you put the card on a sensor and a beep lets you know that the fare has been deducted. You can increase the credit by HK$50 or HK$100 at machines in underground stations or in *7-Eleven* shops. The *Octopus* bonus: you don't have to have loose change with you when you take a bus and can go through the gates at the train stations without buying a ticket. In addition, the MTR grants a reduction. The *Airport Express Travel Pass* for HK\$220 or HK\$300 is not really recommendable; once you deduct the fares for the Airport Express, you will be left with more credit than you could ever use.

IN MACAU

More than 50 bus lines guarantee good connections. Several buses to the islands stop at the Hotel Lisboa (144 C5) *(ᗕ c5)*; almost all of those to 'Barra' (near the Museu Marítimo) (144 B5) *(ᗕ b5)* come close to the city centre. *City tour 3.20 Ptcs, to Taipa 4.20 Ptcs, to Coloane Village 5 Ptcs, to Hac Sa Beach 6.40 Ptcs*

SPORTS & BEACHES

Golf: The only 18-hole golf course open to all is the *Kau Sai Chau Public Golf Course* (139 E3) *(ᗕ 0)*, which can be reached by ferry from Sai Kung. *Bookings: tel. 27 91 33 80 | 18-hole round from HK\$520*
Swimming: There are many beaches in Hong Kong but most are small and lacking in the atmosphere of the South Seas. However, the advantage is that 42 of them are looked after and patrolled by the city. They provide showers, changing rooms, toilets, pontoons and other conveniences that can be used free of charge. Some even have nets to protect bathers

WEATHER IN HONG KONG

	Jan	Feb	March	April	May	June	July	Aug	Sept	Oct	Nov	Dec
Daytime temperatures in °C/°F	18/64	18/64	20/68	24/75	28/82	30/86	31/88	31/88	30/86	27/81	24/75	20/68
Nighttime temperatures in °C/°F	13/55	13/55	16/61	19/66	23/73	26/79	26/79	26/79	25/77	23/73	19/66	15/59
Sunshine hours/day	5	4	3	4	5	5	7	6	7	7	6	6
Precipitation days/month	4	5	7	8	13	18	17	15	12	6	2	3
Water temperatures in °C/°F	18/64	18/64	21/70	24/75	25/77	27/81	28/82	28/82	27/81	26/82	24/75	21/70

from sharks and they are all cleaned regularly and the quality of the water checked. This only applies during the bathing season (April–Oct) but the beaches are accessible throughout the year. As there are no strong currents and little surf, children can also swim safely.

TOURS

The tours of the harbour organised by *Star Ferry* cost from HK$55 *(duration 1 hour | offices at the piers | tel. 6118 62 01 | www. starferry.com.hk/harbourtour). Watertours* offers tours to the Tsing Ma Bridge at HK$230 *(1023A, 10th floor, Star House | 3 Salisbury Rd. | tel. 29 26 38 68 | www.water tours.com.hk)* (130 C6) *(⌖ E9)*.

The ● *Duk Ling (www.dukling.com.hk)*, claimed to be the last sailing junk in Hong Kong, is the most pleasant way to cruise through Victoria Harbour. If you don't want to charter the entire boat, go to the *HKTB office* at the Star Ferry in Tsim Sha Tsui *(tel. 25 08 12 34 | fare HK$100 | take your passport | two tours on both Thursday afternoon and Saturday at noon)*.

Rickshaw Sightseeing Bus offers 'Hop-on-hop-off' tours on two routes on the island *(from 10am, every 30 minutes from the Star Ferry Pier in Central | day ticket HK$50 | tel. 2136 88 88 | www.rickshawbus.com)* as does *Big Bus* with three routes – including one through Kowloon and one to Stanley *(from 10 am from Star Ferry in Central or from the eastern end of the Avenue of Stars in Kowloon | HK$320 for 24 hours., HK$380 for 48 hours | tel. 27 23 21 08 | www.bigbustours.com). Gray Line Tours (Tel. 23 68 71 11 | www.grayline.com.hk)* organises tours of the New Territories.

TAXIS

All taxis are registered and use a taximeter (minimum tariff in the inner city HK$20).

Trips through tunnels cost twice the toll fee because the driver has to drive back. The green taxis in the New Territories do not drive into the city. A double yellow line on the curb shows that no stopping is allowed – this applies to taxis too. A single yellow line indicates that stopping is not permitted during peak traffic hours. Very few taxi drivers understand English. Write the address of your destination in Chinese, if it is not included in this guide, and always have the Chinese name of your hotel with you. The same is true of Macau.

THEATRE & CONCERT TICKETS

Tickets for almost all performances can be ordered from *Cityline (tel. 2111 53 33 | daily 10am–8pm)*. Tickets for events in the Cultural Centre and City Hall can be purchased from their box offices in advance or before performance. *Urbtix (online sales | booking tel. 2111 59 99 | urbtix.cityline. com.hk)* provides information on events in city theatres and halls. Tickets for events in Macau are available under *www.macau ticket.com | tel. in Macau 28 55 55 55 | tel. in Hong Kong 23 80 50 83*.

TIME

Hong Kong Time (HKT) is 8 hours ahead of Greenwich Mean Time, during European summer plus 7 hours, 14 hours behind US Eastern Time (EST) and 3 hours behind Australian Eastern Time (AEST), one hour less during summers daylight saving time.

TIPPING

Most restaurants and bars charge inclusive prices. The change is usually returned on a small tray and it is customary to leave 5–10% of the amount as a tip. Most people round up the taxi fare.

USEFUL PHRASES CANTONESE

IN BRIEF

Yes, correct/	係 [hai]/
Yes, okay	好 [hoe]
No, wrong/	唔係 [m hai/
No, not okay	唔好 [m hoe]
Maybe	可能 [haw nang]
Thank you/	多謝 [daw jeh]/
Nichts zu danken!	唔駛唔該 [m sai m goi]
Excuse me, please	對唔住! [doi m ju]
May I ...?	可唔可以 ...? [haw m haw-yee]
Pardon	你講乜嘢話? [nay gong mat yeh wa]
I would like to .../	我想要 ... [naw sung yiu]/
have you got ...?	有冇 ... [yao moe]
Where is ...?	... 係邊度? [hai bindoe]
How much is ...?	幾多錢? [gay daw tsin]
I like this/	唔錯呀 [m tsaw ah]/
I don't like this	唔係幾好 [m hai gay hoe]
good/bad	好/唔好 [hoe/m hoe]
broken/	壞咗 [wai joe]/
doesn't work	冇反應 [moe fanying]
too much/	多得滯 [dawdak jai]/
much/	好多 [hoe daw]/
little	少少 [syiu-syiu]
all/nothing	全部/全部唔要 [tsinbao/tsinbao m yiu]
Help!/Attention!/	救命!/睇住! [gaomeng/taiju]/
Caution!	小心! [syiu sam]
ambulance	白車 [bak cheh]
police/	差人 [tsai yan]/
fire brigade	消防員 [syiufonyeun]
prohibition/forbidden	唔俾 [m bay]
danger/dangerous	危險 [ai heem]

GREETINGS, FAREWELL

Good morning!/	早晨! [joe san]/
afternoon!	你好! [nay hoe]
Good evening!/night!	早抖! [joe tao]
Hello! (on the phone)	喂! [wai]
My name is ...	我叫 ... [naw gyiu]
What's your name?	你貴姓? [nay gwai sing]
I am ... [American/English]	我係 ... [naw hai]

Do you speak Cantonese?

This guide will help you to say the basic words and phrases in Cantonese

DATE & TIME

Monday/Tuesday	星期一/星期二 [singkay yat/singkay yee]
Wednesday/Thursday	星期三/星期四 [singkay sam/singkay say]
Friday/Saturday	星期五/星期六 [singkay m/singkay lok]
Sunday/	星期天 [singkay teen]/
holiday	工作日 [goong jok teen]
today/tomorrow/	今日/聽日[gammyat/tingyat]/
yesterday	噚日 [tsamyat]
hour/minute	鐘頭/分鐘 [joongtao/fenn joong]
day/night/	日抖/夜晚 [yat tao/ye man]/
week	星期 [singkay]
month/year/	月/年 [yiu/neen]/
Holiday	假期 [gah kay]
What time is it?	幾多點? [gay daw deem]
It's three o'clock	三點 [sam deem]
It's half past three	三點半 [sam deem boon]

TRAVEL

open/	開門 [hoy moon]/
closed	唔開門 [m hoy moon]
entrance	入口 [yap hao]
exit	出口 [tsoot hao]
departure/	開車 [hoy cheh]/
departure (flight)/	起飛 [hay fay]/
arrival	到達 [daw daat]
toilets/restrooms/	洗手間 [sai sho gan]/
ladies/gentlemen	女/男 [noy/nam]
(no) drinking water	(非)飲用水 [(fay) yam yoong soy]
left/right	左邊/右邊 [tsaw been/yao been]
straight ahead/back	直行/回去 [jik hang/wooey hoy]
close/far	遠/近 [yuen/gan]
bus/bus stop	巴士/巴士站 [ba see/ba see jam]
MTR/tram	地鐵/電車 [day tit/deen cheh]
taxi/cab	的士 [dek see]
street map/map	地圖 [day toe]
train station/	火車站 [faw cheh jam]/
pier	碼頭 [ma tao]
airport	機場 [gay chang]
timetable/ticket	時刻表/車飛 [see hak beeou/cheh fay]
single/return	單程/來回 [dan tseng/loy wooey]

USEFUL PHRASES

FOOD & DRINK

The menu, please	餐牌唔該 [tsanpai m goi]
Could I please have ...?	... 唔該 [m goi]
bottle/can/glass	樽/罐/杯 [joon/goon/booey]
knife/fork/spoon/chopstick	刀/叉/匙羹/筷子 [doe/tsah/tsee gang/faidsee]
salt/pepper/sugar/vinegar	鹽/胡椒粉/糖/醋 [yeem/hoo yieu fan/ton/tsoe]
soy sauce/milk/lemon	豉油/牛奶/檸檬 [see yao/ao nai/ning meung]
vegetarian/allergy	素食/敏感 [soe sek/man gam]
May I have the bill, please?	唔該你埋單 [m goi nay mai dan]
bill/receipt/tip	帳單/收條/貼士 [jeung dan/sao tieu/tip see]

SHOPPING

pharmacy/chemist	藥房 [ye fong]/Watson's
baker/market	麵包鋪/街市 [min bao paw/gai see]
shopping centre/department store/supermarket	購物中心/百貨公司/超級市場 [cao mat joong sam/bak foe goong see/tsiu kap see tsun]
camera shop/newsagent	影視鋪/報攤 [ying see paw/boe taan]
100 grammes/1 kilo	一百克/一公斤 [yat bak hak/yat goonggan]
expensive/cheap/price	貴得滯/平/價錢 [gwai/peng/gatseen]
more/less	多/少 [doe/syiu]

BANKS, MONEY & CREDIT CARDS

bank/ATM	銀行/柜員機 [nan hong/gwai yeung gay]
pin code	密碼 [mat ma], PIN

NUMBERS

0	零 [ling]	15	十五 [sap m]
1	一 [yat]	16	十六 [sap lok]
2	二 [yee]	17	十七 [sap tsat]
Two of those 兩個 [leunggoe]		18	十八 [sap bat]
3	三 [sam]	19	十九 [sap gao]
4	四 [say]	20	二十 [yee sap]
5	五 [m]	70	七十 [chat sap]
6	六 [look]	80	八十 [baat-ssap]
7	七 [tsat]	90	九十 [gao sap]
8	八 [bat]	100	一百 [yat bak]
9	九 [gao]	200	二百 [yee bak]
10	十 [sap]	1000	一千 [yat chin]
11	十一 [sap yat]	2000	兩千 [leung tseen]
12	十二 [sap yee]	10 000	一萬 [yat man]
13	十三 [sap sam]	½	一半 [yat boon]
14	十四 [sap say]	¼	四分一 [say fan yat]

NOTES

FOR YOUR NEXT HOLIDAY ...

MARCO POLO TRAVEL GUIDES

ALGARVE
AMSTERDAM
AUSTRALIA
BANGKOK
BARCELONA
BERLIN
BRUSSELS
BUDAPEST
CALIFORNIA
CAPE TOWN
    WINE LANDS,
    GARDEN ROUTE
COLOGNE
CORFU
GRAN CANARIA
CRETE
CUBA
CYPRUS
    NORTH AND
    SOUTH
DUBAI

DUBROVNIK &
    DALMATIAN COAST
EDINBURGH
EGYPT
FINLAND
FLORIDA
FRENCH RIVIERA
    NICE, CANNES &
    MONACO
HONGKONG
    MACAU
IRELAND
ISRAEL
ISTANBUL
JORDAN
KOS
LAKE GARDA

LANZAROTE
LAS VEGAS
LONDON
LOS ANGELES
MADEIRA
    PORTO SANTO
MALLORCA
MALTA
    GOZO
MOROCCO
NEW YORK
NEW ZEALAND
NORWAY
PARIS
RHODES

ROME
SAN FRANCISCO
SICILY
SOUTH AFRICA
STOCKHOLM
TENERIFE
THAILAND
TURKEY
    SOUTH COAST
UNITED ARAB
    EMIRATES
VENICE
VIETNAM

- PACKED WITH INSIDER TIPS
- BEST WALKS AND TOURS
- FULL-COLOUR PULL-OUT MAP
  AND STREET ATLAS

STREET ATLAS

The green line [____] indicates the Walking tours (p. 100–105)

All tours are also marked on the pull-out map

Photo: The shore promenade in Kowloon with a view of Hong Kong Island

Exploring Hong Kong

The map on the back cover shows how the area has been sub-divided

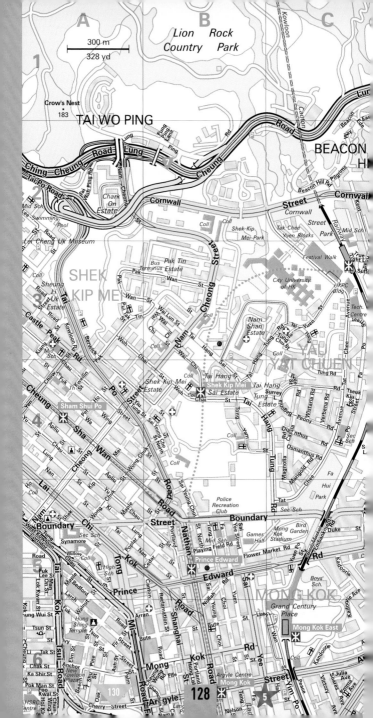

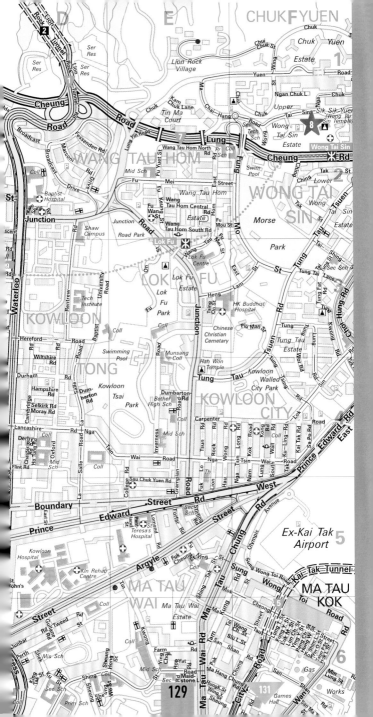

Grid references: D, E, F (top), with numbered rows 1–6 (right side)

Streets and places

CHUK YUEN — Chuk Yuen Estate, Chuk Yuen Road

Lion Rock Village
Ser Res
Cheung Road
Lion Rock Tunnel
Broadcast Drive
Marconi
Fessenden Rd
Kam Chuk Lane
Chai-Hang
Tin Ma Court
Chuk Yuen
Ngan Chuk L
Sik Sik Yuen (Wong Tai Sin Temple)
Wong Tai Sin Estate
Upper Wong Tai Sin Estate

WANG TAU HOM — Wang Tau Hom North, Wang Tau Hom Central, Wang Tau Hom South Rd
Fu Mei Sch
Wang Fu Kwong St
Fu Wang St
Lung Tech Sch
Lung Cheung Rd
Swim Pool

WONG TAI SIN — Wong Tai Sin Rd, Lower Wong Tai Sin Estate
China St
Sheung Fung St
Morse Park
Tsz Wan Shan

Baptist Hospital
Junction Road Park
Shaw Campus
Junction Road

LOK FU — Lok Fu Centre, Lok Fu Estate, Lok Fu Park
Fu Tung St
Wang Tung St
Heng Lam St
Piu Man St
HK Buddhist Hospital

KOWLOON TONG
University Road
Baptist Coll
Tech Institute
Renfrew Road
Hereford Road
Wiltshire
Durham Rd
Hampshire Rd
Selkirk Rd
Moray Rd
Cambridge
Lancashire Rd
Derby Rd
Oxford Rd
Flint Rd
Waterloo Road
Kowloon Tsai Park
Swimming Pool
Dumbarton Rd
La Salle Road
Inverness Rd
Wai Road
Sau Chuk Yuen Road
Nga Tsin Wai Road
Grampian Road

Chinese Christian Cemetery
Munsang Coll
Hah Won Temple
Dumbarton
Bethel High Sch
Carpenter Rd

KOWLOON CITY
Kowloon Walled City Park
Tung Tau Estate
Tsuen Wan
Kowloon City Rd
Prince Edward Road East
Prince Edward Road West
Tsun Fuk St
Lung Kong Rd
Kai Tak Rd
Nga Tsin Wong Rd
Sa Po Rd
Nam Kok Rd
Lion Rock Rd
Lung Shing Rd
Lok Shan Rd

St Teresa's Hospital
Kowloon Hospital
Kln Rehab Centre
St John's
Boundary Street
Prince Edward Rd
Argyle Street
Fuk Ching Coll
Farfar St

MA TAU WAI — Ma Tau Wai Estate, Ma Tau Wai Rd
Ma Tau Chung Rd
Chung Hau St
Sung Wong Toi Rd

MA TAU KOK — Ma Tau Kok Road
Ex-Kai Tak Airport
Kai Tak Tunnel
Olympic Avenue
Gas Works
Games Hall
Min Lung St

Gilman Rd
Tweed St
Perth St
King Ku St
Ma Hang Chung Rd
Ha Heung Rd
Mok Cheong St
Shing Tak St
San Shan Rd

129 131

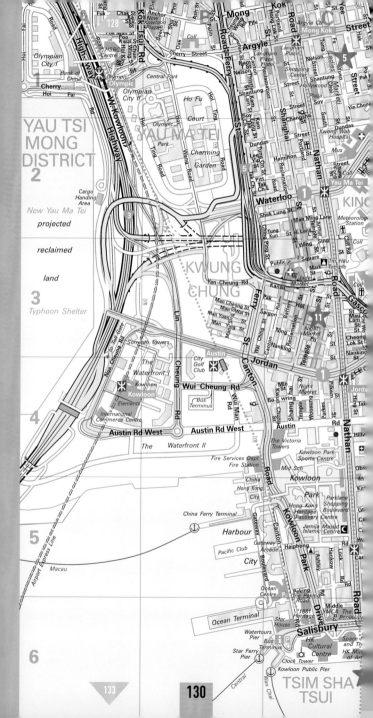

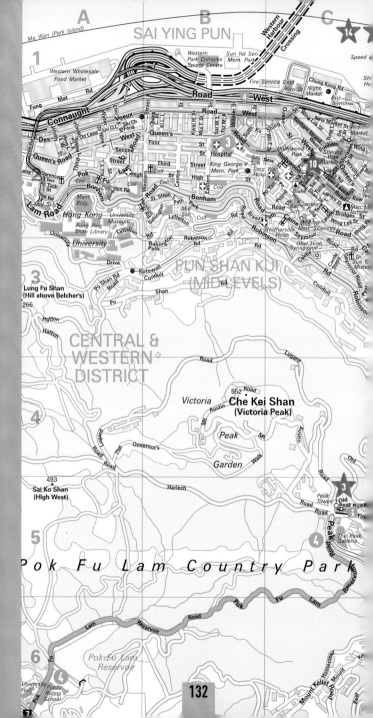

Ma Wan (Park Island)

A   B   C

1

Western Wholesale
Food Market

Western
Park Complex
Sports Centre

Sun Yat Sen
Mem. Park

Western Harbour
Crossing

Speed

Fung Mat Rd

Fire Service Dept
Fire St.

Chung Kong Rd

Connaught   Road   West

Des   Voeux

Queen's Road   West

Second
Street

First   Street

Third   Street

High   Street

Bonham

King George V
Mem. Park

NOHO

Hospital

Hollywood
Road

Man Mo
Temple

Lam Road

Hong Kong
University

Fung Ping
Shan Library

University
Museum

Lyttelton   Rd

Robinson   Rd

Robinson

Nethersole
Hosp

Hong Kong Med.
Sciences

Ohel Leah
Synagogue

Seymour

Conduit

Castle

Robinson

3

Lung Fu Shan
(Hill above Belcher's)
266

Kotewall
Conduit

PUN SHAN KUI
(MID-LEVELS)

Po Shan Rd

Hatton

Hatton

CENTRAL &
WESTERN
DISTRICT

Road

Lugard

4

493
Sai Ko Shan
(High West)

Victoria
Peak

552   Road
Che Kei Shan
(Victoria Peak)

Austin

Peak

Governor's

Garden

Walk

Harlech

Austin

Old

Peak
Tower

Old
Peak Road

The Peak
Galleria

3

1   Fin

4

5

Pok Fu Lam Country Park

Reservoir

Pok   Fu   Lam

Road

Lam   Reservoir

6

Pok Fu Lam
Reservoir

University
Hall

Public
Riding
School

Mount Keller

Mount

Peak

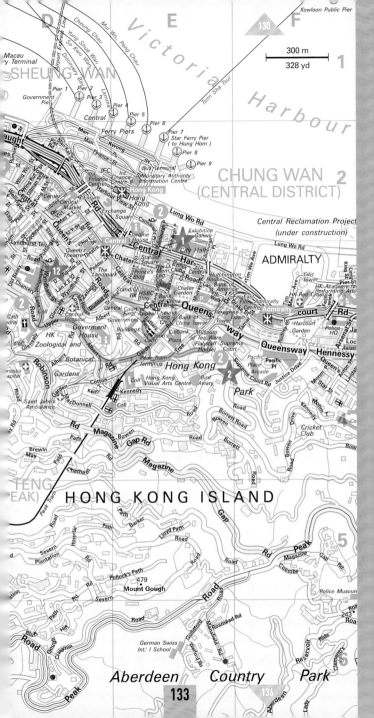

Kowloon Public Pier

Victoria

130

Macau
Ferry Terminal

Cheung Chau
Mui Wo, Peng Chau
Airport Express Line
Yung Shue Wan
Discovery Bay
So Kwu Wan

300 m
328 yd

1

SHEUNG WAN

Pier 1 Pier 2 Pier 3 Pier 4
Government
Pier
Central
Ferry Piers
Pier 5
Pier 6
Pier 7
Star Ferry Pier
(to Hung Hom)
Pier 8
Pier 9

Harbour

Tsim Sha Tsui

Man Kwong St

Int'l Bus Terminal
Monetary Authority
Information Centre

CHUNG WAN
(CENTRAL DISTRICT)

2

naught

IFC
Int'l
Finance
Centre
The
Center
Int'l
Finance
Centre II
Harbour View St
Hong Kong
Exchange
Square

Hong Kong

Central Reclamation Project
(under construction)

Central

Jardine
House

Lung Wo Rd

Lung Wo Rd

ADMIRALTY

Exhibition
Gallery
City Hall

Des Voeux
Central
Central Market
The Forum

Wing
Connaught Rd
Man
Finance St

Queen's
Pottinger
Theatre
Pedder St
Chater Rd
The Landmark
Lan Kwai Fong
Wyndham

12

Statue
Square
Prince's
Bldg

City Hall

Citic
Tower

HK Academy
for Performing Arts
HK Red Cross

Legislative
Council

Bank of
America

Pier St

Central

Central
Court
Final Appeal
Court
Government
Buildings

HSBC
Bldg
Standard
Chartered
Bank

2

Cheung
Kong
Centre

St John's
Cath

Citibank
Plaza

Bank of
China Tower

Far East
Finance
Centre
Lippo

Hutchinson
House
Bank of
America

Harcourt
Garden

Peregrine
Tower

Admiralty

Police
HQ

Hennessy Rd

Central

Queen's
way

Queensway

HK
Zoological and
Botanical
Gardens

Robinson Rd

Government
House

Albert
Rd

Peak Tram
Terminus

Museum
of Tea Ware
(Flagstaff
House)

Court of
Final Appeal
Supreme
Court

Hong Kong

2

Supreme Court Rd

Queensway

Pacific
Place
Arcade

Pacific
Place

2

Park

Justice Drive

Saint John's
Ambulance

MacDonnell

Cotton
Rd
Kennedy

Bird
Aviary

Hong Kong
Visual Arts Centre

Road

Road

Cricket
Club

Borrett Road

Brewin
May
Path

Chatha St

Bowen
Gap Rd

Magazine

Magazine

Road

Bowen
Road

Borrett
Road

Bowen
Drive

Kennedy
Rd

TENG
PEAK)

Peak Tram

HONG KONG ISLAND

Gap

5

Severn
Plantation
Rd

Path

Barker

Lloyd Path

Rd

Road

Road

Road

Peak Rd

Magazine
Coombe

Gap Rd

Police Museum

479
Mount Gough

Pollock's Path

Severn

Road

Road

Guildford

Rosmead Rd

Reservoir

Rd

243
Road

Bluff
Road

Plunkett's Rd

German Swiss
Int'l School

Mansfield Rd

Watford Rd

Clementi's

Peak

Aberdeen Country Park

Aberdeen

133

136

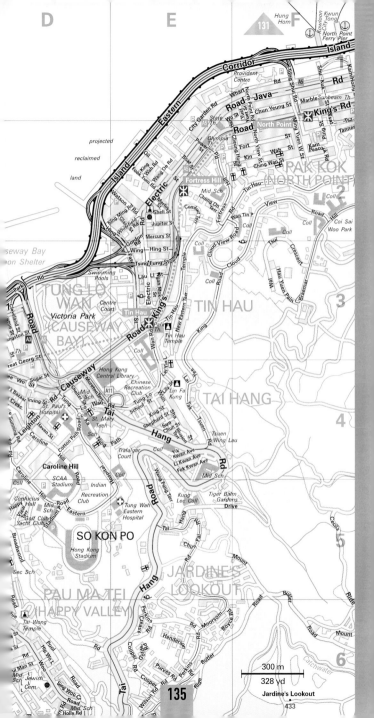

131

Hung Hom
Kwun Tong
Kowloon City
North Point
Ferry Pier

Island

Corridor

Provident Centre

Eastern

Island

Road

Java

Road

King's Rd

North Point

PAK KOK
NORTH POINT

projected
reclaimed
land

Electric

King's

Fortress Hill

Mid Sch

TIN HAU

seway Bay
on Shelter

Swimming
Pools

Road

TUNG LO
WAN
(CAUSEWAY
BAY)

Victoria Park

Tin Hau

Centre
Court

Tin Hau
Temple

Causeway

Road

TAI HANG

Hong Kong
Central Library

Chinese
Recreation
Club

Lin Fa
Kung

Tai
Hang

St Paul's
Hospital

St Mary
Tech

Leighton

Caroline

Caroline Hill

SCAA
Stadium

Indian
Recreation
Club

Trafalgar
Court

Yik Kwan Ave
Li Kwan Ave
Fuk Kwan Ave

Mid Sch

Tung Wah
Eastern
Hospital

Kung
Lee Coll

Tiger Balm
Gardens
Drive

SO KON PO

Hong Kong
Stadium

Road

JARDINE'S
LOOKOUT

PAU MA TEI
(HAPPY VALLEY)

Tai Wong
Temple

Jewish
Cem

Mount

Catchwater

300 m
328 yd

Jardine's Lookout

433

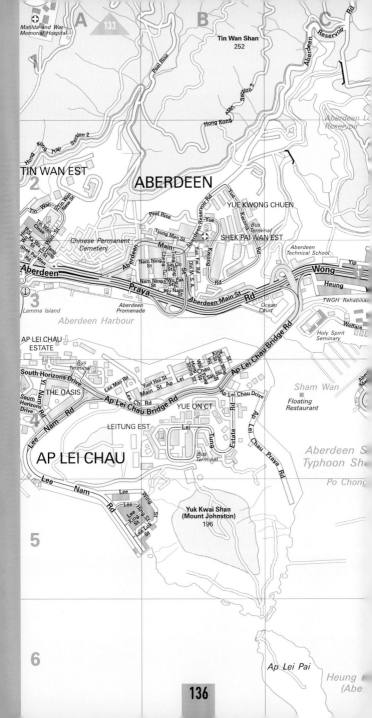

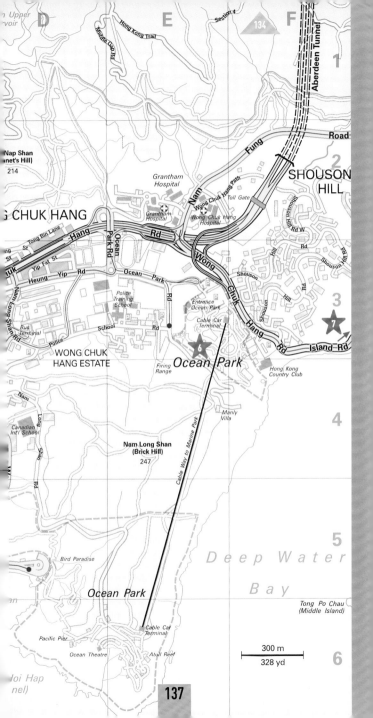

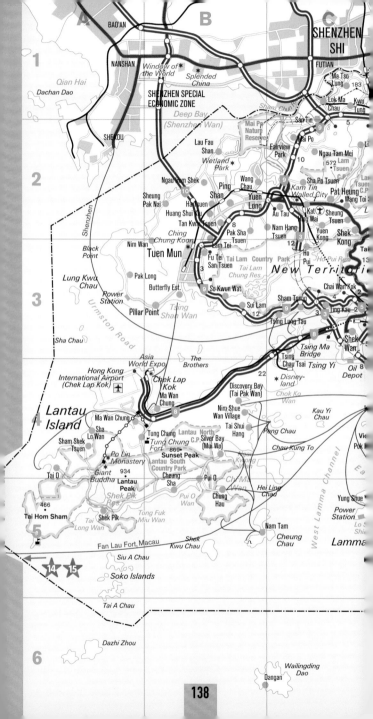

HONG KONG
Special Administrative Region

South China Sea
(Nam Hai)

139

This index lists a selection of the streets and squares shown in the street atlas

This index lists a selection of the streets and squares shown in the street atlas

E
F

1

2

3

4

5

6

Border Checkpoint

Avenida Norte
do Hipódromo

Avenida da

Ponte de Amizade

Avenida da Amizade

Ponte de Amizade

Ponte de Amizade

Pearl

Areia
Preta

Nossa Senhora
Fatima

R. dos Hortelãos
R. da Tranquilidade
Av. do Hipódromo
R. do Hipódromo
R. Direita do Hipódromo
R. do Mercado
R. da
St Joseph
The Worker
Estr. Marginal do
Hipódromo
Rua de Maio
Rua de Maio
Avenida
Canal Novo
Nordeste

R. da
R. da
R. Um do
Bairro Iao Hon
R. do
Iao Hon
R. Dois do Iao Hon
R. de Iao Hon
Av. Coronel
Mesquita
Estr. Marginal do Canal Novo
Av. do Coronel Mesquita
Rua
da Areia Preta
R. de Areia Preta
Av. do Francisco Vieira Machado
Ma Kau
Seak
de
Maio

Av. de Venceslau Morais
Rampa dos Cavaleiros
Estrada de Ferreira do Amaral
Estr. do Repouso
Rua dos Pescadores

Our Lady of Piety
Cemetery
Montanha Russa
Garden
Estrada de Dom
Maria II
Museum of
Communication

Kun
Iam

Lin Zexu
Mem. Mus.
Wong Ha
Park
Mong-Ha
Fort

Reservoir

Istmo
de Ferreira do Amaral
Estr.
do Arco

Ramalhete Barbosa
as Portas
do Cerco
Barrier
Gate

Cable Car

Flora
Garden
Dr. Sun Yat Sen
Mem. House

Guia Hill
Municipal
Park

Estr. do Reservatório

Cachaças

Rodrigues

Avenida

da
Amizade
Grand Prix Stand

Macau
Ferry Terminal

Heliport

Macau Palace
Casino

Guia Tunnel

Guia Fort and
Lighthouse

Estr.
Eng. Trigo

Estrada

Grand Prix
Museum
Macau
Forum

Golden
Lotus Flower

Fisherman's
Wharf

Outer Harbour

Rua
de Malaca

Rodrigo

Dr.
do

Luís
de
Gonzaga Gomes

Alameda Dr. Carlos d'Assumpção

Av. Dr. Sun Yat Sen

Amizade

Av. do Governador
Jaime Silvério Marques

Rua de Berlim

Av. Xian
Xing Hai

Handover
Gifts Museum

Art
Museum

Macau
Cultural Centre

Sen

Kun Iam
Statue

Macau
Science Centre

Ponte de Amizade

Hong Kong

Sir Anders Ljungstedt
24 de Junho
R. de

Grand

Yat

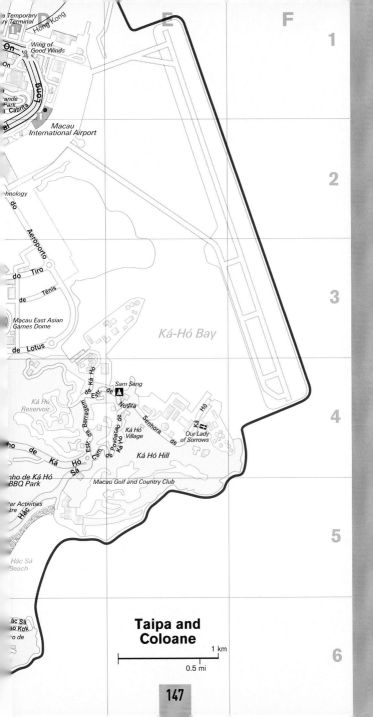

D **E** **F**

1

a Temporary ry Terminal
Hong Kong

Wing of Good Winds

Ón

ande Park Cabrita

Macau International Airport

2

hnology

do

Aeroporto

do Tiro

de Ténis

Macau East Asian Games Dome

de Lotus

3

Ká-Hó Bay

Ká Hó Reservoir

Sam Seng

de Ká Hó

Nostra

Barragem

Estr.

Povoação

de Ká Hó

Senhora

Ká Ho

de

Ká Hó Village

Our Lady of Sorrows

de

ho de Ká

Ká Hó Hill

Sá

Cam.

4

nho de Ká Hó BBQ Park

Macau Golf and Country Club

ter Activities tre Hác

5

Hác Sá Beach

ác Sá ão Kok ro de

Taipa and Coloane

1 km

0.5 mi

6

147

KEY TO STREET ATLAS

四車道公路 Vierspurige Straße		Road with four lanes Route à quatre voies
遠程公路 Fernstraße -, auf Hochbrücke		Trunk road -, on elevated road Route à grande circulation -, surélevée
主要公路 Hauptstraße		Main road Route principale
其它公路 Sonstige Straßen		Other roads Autres routes
單行公路 – 信息 Einbahnstraße - Information		One way road - Information Rue à sens unique - Information
步行區 Fußgängerzone		Pedestrian zone Zone piétonne
主要鐵路干綫, 火車站 Hauptbahn mit Bahnhof		Main railway with station Chemin de fer principal avec gare
其他鐵路干綫 Sonstige Bahn		Other railway Autre ligne
地下鐵道 U-Bahn		Mass Transit Railway Métro
有軌電車 Straßenbahn		Tramway Tramway
海運綫–停靠站 Schifffahrtslinie mit Anlegestelle		Ferry with pier Ligne maritime avec embarcadère
寺廟–寺願,風景區 Tempel - Sehenswerter Tempel		Temple - Temple of interest Temple - Temple remarquable
清真寺 – 教堂 Moschee - Kirche		Mosque - Church Mosquée - Église
紀念碑 – 猶太教堂 Denkmal - Synagoge		Monument - Synagogue Monument - Synagogue
荅 – 青年旅社 Turm - Jugendherberge		Tower - Youth hostel Tour - Auberge de Jeunesse
警察局 – 郵局 Polizeistation - Postamt		Police station - Post office Poste de police - Bureau de poste
醫院 Krankenhaus		Hospital Hôpital
建築, 公共建築 Bebaute Fläche, öffentliches Gebäude		Built-up area, public building Zones bâties, edifice public
工業區 Industriegelände		Industrial area Zone industrielle
公園, 森林 Park, Wald		Park, forest Parc, bois
徒步觀光路線 Stadtspaziergänge		Walking tours Promenades en ville
MARCO POLO Highlight		MARCO POLO Highlight

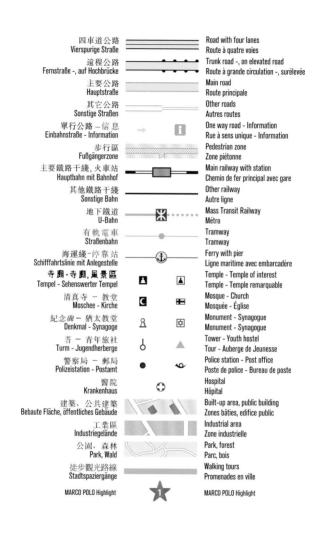

INDEX

This index lists all sights, museums, and destinations in this guide. Numbers in bold indicate a main entry. Destinations in Macau are marked (MA).

WRITE TO US

e-mail: info@marcopologuides.co.uk

Did you have a great holiday?
Is there something on your mind?
Whatever it is, let us know!
Whether you want to praise, alert us
to errors or give us a personal tip –
MARCO POLO would be pleased to
hear from you.
We do everything we can to provide the
very latest information for your trip.

Nevertheless, despite all of our authors'
thorough research, errors can creep in.
MARCO POLO does not accept any
liability for this. Please contact us by
e-mail or post.

MARCO POLO Travel Publishing Ltd
Pinewood, Chineham Business Park
Crockford Lane, Chineham
Basingstoke, Hampshire RG24 8AL
United Kingdom

PICTURE CREDITS
Cover photograph: Neon lights and advertising signs in Hong Kong (Getty Images/Digital Vision: Adams)
DuMont Bildarchiv: Riehle (108, 108/109); R. Freyer (9, 21, 25, 30, 32, 36, 38, 40, 43, 53, 59, 69, 73, 88/89, 90, 103, 105, 106); Getty Images/Digital Vision: Adams (1 top); R. Hackenberg (109); T. Haltner (2 centre bottom, 26/27, 34, 44, 46, 63); Huber: Borchi (96), Cozzi (6, 12/13, 76/77), Eisele-Hein (2 top, 5, 18/19), Gräfenhain (front flap right, 10/11, 126/127, 149), Huber (78); © iStockphoto.com: Chan Chun Tak (17 bottom), ivanmateev (16 top); Laif: Celentano (60 left), Lengler (99), Riehle (106/107); Christina Lee (16 bottom); mauritius images: age (61), Alamy (2 centre top, 2 bottom, 3 top, 4, 7, 14, 24 left, 24 right, 48, 54/55, 56, 60 right, 64/65, 66, 71, 87, 100/101, 112 top, 112 bottom, 113), Harding (85), Vidler (front flap left); mauritius images/Imagebroker: Tack (3 bottom, 8, 80/81, 82); Mountain Yam: Timothy Leung (16 centre); C. Nowak (93, 95, 107); Para/Site Art Space: Joo Choon-Lin (17 top); G. Reichelt (23); H.-W. Schütte (1 bottom); T. Stankiewicz (51); White Star: Gumm (3 centre, 74/75)

1st Edition 2013
Worldwide Distribution: Marco Polo Travel Publishing Ltd, Pinewood, Chineham Business Park,
Crockford Lane, Basingstoke, Hampshire RG24 8AL, United Kingdom. Email: sales@marcopolouk.com
© MAIRDUMONT GmbH & Co. KG, Ostfildern
Chief editors: Michaela Lienemann (concept, managing editor), Marion Zorn (concept, text editor)
Author: Dr. Hans-Wilm Schütte; editor: Corinna Walkenhorst
Programme supervision: Anita Dahlinger, Ann-Katrin Kutzner, Nikolai Michaelis
Picture editor: Gabriele Forst
What's hot: wunder media, Munich
Cartography street atlas: © MAIRDUMONT, Ostfildern; Cartography pull-out map: © MAIRDUMONT, Ostfildern
Design: milchhof : atelier, Berlin; Front cover, pull-out map cover, page 1: factor product munich
Translated from German by Robert Scott McInnes; editor of the English edition: Christopher Wynne
Prepress: M. Feuerstein, Wigel
Phrase book: Dr. Hans-Wilm Schütte, in cooperation with Ernst Klett Sprachen GmbH, Stuttgart, Editorial by Pons Wörterbücher

DOS & DON'TS

A few things you should bear in mind in Hong Kong

DO BE CAREFUL BUYING ELECTRONIC EQUIPMENT

You want to buy a camera, compare prices and then decide on the really special deal only to notice later that the guarantee is just valid in Hong Kong or that, instead of the quality lens, a cheaper one was palmed off on you. The best thing is not to even consider buying goods that seem amazingly cheap. Nobody sells anything below cost. Being sceptical is not enough because it is very difficult to see through the tricks a dealer works with. That is also why you should never do your expensive shopping on the last day in Hong Kong.

DON'T GO ON A ONE-DAY TRIP ACROSS THE BORDER

Short trips across the border to Shenzhen, Canton and Macau are usually more stress than pleasure. There is no relation between the result and the costs and effort involved. Canton is definitely worth a visit but only if you stay for at least one night. This also applies to Macau; it is often underestimated as a destination but you will need longer than just the normal day trip if you really want to soak up the atmosphere.

DON'T FOLLOW TOUTS

This only applies to men, especially if they are alone. Ladies stand outside dubious bars in Wan Chai on the lookout for clients. A poster promises cheap beer. And the beer actually is cheap; but the short chat with the scantily clad barmaid, or the drink for the hostess who sits down at your table, is much more expensive and can put quite a dent in your budget. And, protesting won't help. There is always a price list hanging in an out-of-the-way place and the fleeced man has to cough up.

DO GO FOR THE SLOWER FERRIES

The new ferries to the other islands are perfect for commuters but completely unattractive for tourists. They don't have a sundeck and are expensive. You can't even really look out of the windows. If at all possible, take one of the big, old, slow ferries. That way, you will be able to take in the panorama of Hong Kong from the open top deck at the stern.

DON'T GO ON EXCURSIONS AT WEEKENDS

If the weather is fine, half of Hong Kong pours into any available means of transport on Saturday afternoon and heads for the great outdoors. If you do the same, you will have to queue up wherever you go, will probably have just as little space at the beach as in town, and have to pay expensive weekend surcharges. Take a walk in the parks on Hong Kong Island instead. The same applies to trips to Macau and then you will even have the additional problem of getting back on Sunday evening.